# KNOWING HORSES

to: Izzy

# KNOWING
# HORSES

*Q&As to Boost Your Equine IQ*

LES SELLNOW & CAROL A. BUTLER

*Illustrations by Elara Tanguy*

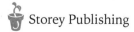 Storey Publishing

*The mission of Storey Publishing is to serve our customers by
publishing practical information that encourages
personal independence in harmony with the environment.*

Edited by Lisa H. Hiley
Art direction and book design by Cynthia N. McFarland
Cover design by Alethea Morrison
Text production by Jennifer Jepson Smith

Illustrations by © Elara Tanguy
Cover photograph by © Mark J. Barrett
Wyoming license plate reproduced with permission from the State of Wyoming

Indexed by Nancy D. Wood

**Storey Publishing**
210 MASS MoCA Way
North Adams, MA 01247
*www.storey.com*

Printed in the United States by Versa Press
10   9   8   7   6   5   4   3   2   1

**LIBRARY OF CONGRESS CATALOGING-IN-PUBLICATION DATA**

Sellnow, Les.
 Knowing horses / by Les Sellnow and Carol A. Butler.
    p. cm.
 Includes index.
 ISBN 978-1-60342-798-2 (pbk. : alk. paper)
 1. Horses. 2. Horses—Behavior. 3. Horses—Training.
 4. Horses—History. I. Butler, Carol A., 1943– II. Title.
 SF285.S436 2012
 636.1—dc23
                          2012013933

# CONTENTS

This book is dedicated to the concerned horse owners and trainers who through the years have stopped "breaking" horses and substituted gentle persuasion in a kind and compassionate manner.

Thanks to Frank Vigilante for suggesting to Carol that she write a book about horses and for helping her to find Les as a co-author. We enjoyed working together to create this book, and we thank our agent, Deirdre Mullane, and our editor, Lisa Hiley, for helping us get to the finish line.

# CHAPTER ONE

# HORSE 101

# A Few Equine Essentials

Over many thousands of years, horses have provided human-kind with food, transportation, mobility, speed, and strength. They shaped our history by allowing people to spread around the globe, helping us become farmers and herders, and bringing us into the Industrial Age. But beyond the purely practical, the human imagination has always been captured by the grace, beauty, and spirit of the horse. Something elemental and deeply emotional draws us to them, inspiring artists, poets, and anyone who is intrigued by the otherness of animals.

## Q Exactly what is a horse, anyway?

**A** A horse is an **ungulate, herbivorous quadruped,** which basically means it has hooves, eats grass, and has four legs. The present-day *Equus ferus caballus* is the only remaining subspecies of the formerly large and complex family called *Equidae*. Over the past 60 million years, the horse has evolved from a fox-sized, multi-toed creature into the large, single-toed animal found throughout the world in different colors and sizes. (See *When did horses first appear on earth?*, page 205.)

## Q Is there more than one species of equine?

**A** The approximately 300 breeds of horses and ponies worldwide all belong to the same species, *Equus caballus*. Donkeys and asses are a different species, *E. asinus*. Mules are a hybrid of these two, not a separate species. The only true wild horse, the Przewalski Horse, is in a class by itself: *E. ferus Przewalski*. (See *The Last Truly Wild Horse*, page 192.) Then there are zebras (see the facing page).

**FAST FACT** The quagga, a subspecies of the plains zebra once found in southern Africa, was hunted to extinction in the late nineteenth century.

*From tiny* Eohippus *to modern* Equus, *the horse has come a long way. Horses are in the family Perissodactyla, or "odd-toed ungulates," which makes them related to rhinoceroses and tapirs.*

## A HORSE BY ANY OTHER NAME

A horse is a horse, of course, of course, but depending on his gender and age, he might be called something else.

**Foal.** A horse of either sex who is less than 1 year old.

**Weanling.** A foal who is still nursing from his dam. Most horses are weaned between 4 and 6 months of age.

**Yearling.** A horse in the second year of his life.

**Filly.** A young female horse; in most countries, including the United States, a filly is 4 years old or less. In the United Kingdom and a few other countries, fillies can be up to 5 years old.

**Colt.** A young male horse under the age of 4.

**Mare.** An adult female horse.

**Broodmare.** An adult female horse primarily used to produce foals.

**Stallion.** An uncastrated adult male horse over the age of 4.

**Gelding.** A male horse (or donkey or mule) who has been castrated to modify potentially aggressive, sexually driven behavior.

## Q Are zebras equines?

**A** Yes. Zebras belong to the species *E. zebra*. East Africa is home to very large migratory herds of plains zebras, as well as some endangered Grevy's zebras. Mountain zebras, also endangered, are found in southern and southwestern Africa. The three subspecies of *E. zebra* rarely interbreed successfully. (See: *Why don't you ever see anyone riding a zebra?*, page 14; *Black and White and Black All Over*, page 15.)

## Q Do horses have elbows and knees?

**A** The equine elbow is part of the joint structure connecting the humerus with the radius, just below the chest (see illustration on the next page). A horse's elbow can't be compared to a human elbow

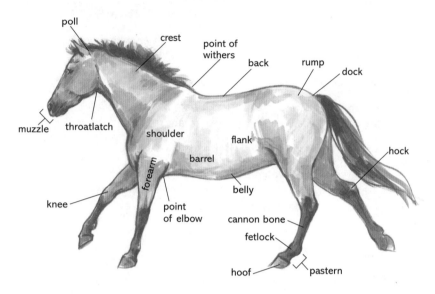

(its elbow and its knee are on the same limb), but some parts of the equine skeleton are similar. For example, the equine radius that runs from knee to fetlock is comparable to the radius that runs from a human's elbow to wrist.

The bones in a horse's knee are similar to the bones in the human wrist. A horse's metacarpal bones along each side of the radius are comparable to the bones in a human's palm, and the three phalanges that comprise the bones that run from the fetlock into a horse's foot are somewhat like the bones in a human's fingers.

FAST FACT **Horses have no muscles in their lower legs, only tendons and ligaments.**

## Q How long can a horse live?

A Horses in the wild have a natural lifespan of about 18 years. With good nutrition and proper care, a domestic horse can be lively and productive well into its twenties or longer. Some breeds, such as Arabians, Haflingers, and Lipizzans, tend to live longer than others. Shetland ponies are also known for longevity, frequently reaching 30 years of age and more.

## Q Why are horses measured in hands, not feet?

**A** Horses are traditionally described as standing a certain number of hands high. Each hand represents 4 inches (10 cm), the width of an average human hand (presumably male). Horses are measured from the top of the withers (the ridge between the shoulder blades that is the tallest point of the body) to the ground. A 14-hand horse, for example, stands 56 inches (142 cm) at the withers; one who is 15.2 hands stands 62 inches (158 cm).

Note that the decimal in these measurements does not indicate a fraction of the total measurement. The number before the decimal indicates the total number of full hands; the number after the decimal indicates the additional number of inches.

*A small pony may measure 11 hands or less, while an unusually large horse can measure more than 20 hands. The average height for most breeds is between 14 and 16 hands, with weights ranging from 800 to 1,200 pounds (363–544 kg). (See* What is the largest breed of horse? The smallest?, *page 84.)*

# Congratulations — It's a Bay!

**THE BASIC HORSE COLORS** are brown, black, and gray, but a large range of shades exists within those categories. Some colors have black points, which are the mane and tail, lower legs, and tips of the ears.

**Bay.** Bays are brown with black points. The coat color can be a deep tan, a rich reddish brown, or mahogany.

**Bay roan.** The base color is bay with white hairs mixed in. The legs, head, mane, and tail are usually darker.

**Black.** A true black horse is rare, but will normally have dark brown eyes and black skin. Some horses retain their deep black hue year round, but most black coats fade toward brown if exposed to a lot of sunlight.

**Blue roan.** A combination of black and white hairs creates a bluish coat with black points.

**Brown.** Brown horses can range from very light to nearly black. Most brown horses have black manes and tails, but they differ from bays in that the muzzles, eyebrows, quarters, and flanks may be reddish or golden brown (also called mealy).

**Buckskin.** The ideal buckskin is the color of tanned deerhide, but the coat can be any clear shade from yellow to dark gold. The skin is black and the points are black or dark brown. Some buckskins have a dorsal stripe. (See Dun.)

**Chestnut.** Ranging from reddish gold to deep copper, chestnut horses have a mane and tail either the same color as or lighter than the coat. They have dark brown eyes and black skin, though no black hairs. They may have pink skin under any white areas.

**Cremello.** Cream-colored body with white tail and mane, pinkish skin, and blue eyes.

**Dun.** Similar to buckskin, but often described as "smutty" because the individual hairs are more deeply pigmented. Most duns sport a dorsal stripe down their backs and may have stripes on their shoulders and legs. Their tails and manes are always darker than their coats, and they usually have darker faces and legs.

**Gray.** Gray horses are born a dark base color and become whiter as they mature. The adult hair is white or dappled, or a combination of white mingled with other colors. Grays normally have black skin and dark eyes.

> *Genetically, there is no such thing as an albino horse. By definition, an albino has no pigment and lacks coat color; the eyes and skin are pink. A true white horse has pink skin but the eyes are always blue or brown.*

Dappled or freckled coats are usually in the process of changing to a lighter gray that may eventually appear white. (See White.)

**Grulla (also grullo).** An intense color that can vary from light gray to smoky gray, this shade is sometimes called mouse-colored. Unlike a gray horse, however, there are no white hairs in the mix, and grullas have dorsal and shoulder striping, as well as barring on the legs and a darker head.

**Palomino.** This prized color ranges from pale yellow (almost white) to bright gold and includes light tan and deep chestnut, known as chocolate. The mane and tail are lighter than the coat, often flaxen (white).

**Perlino.** This color is much like the cremello, but the points are darker, usually rust or orange. Perlinos normally have pink skin and blue eyes.

**Pinto.** Multicolored coat with patches of brown and white or black and white. There are many variations of this coat color, characterized in some cases by the shape and location of the patches.

**Red dun.** This color includes a wide range of reddish hues with somewhat darker points and a distinct dorsal stripe; the stripes are usually red, never black.

**Red roan (also strawberry roan).** The base color is chestnut with white hair mixed in.

**Roan.** A pattern with an even mixture of white and colored hairs on the body but with solid-colored points. Unlike gray horses, roans do not lighten with age, though their coats may change seasonally. (See also Bay roan, Blue roan, and Red roan.)

**Sorrel.** A Western term for "chestnut" (see facing page).

**White.** A white horse is quite rare, with most "white" horses actually being gray. True whites are born with white hair and pink skin. They can have either brown or blue eyes. The coat remains white throughout the horse's lifetime.

**Q** Can a horse have chrome, like a car?

**A** Rather than metal highlights, chrome on a horse refers to white markings. Leg markings are called socks or stockings, depending on the length, but if the legs are white from hoof to knee, the horse is said to have a lot of chrome. Some horses will have added chrome such as a blaze of white down the forehead and face. (See *Stars and Strips Forever*, below.)

> **FAST FACT** The "points" of a horse are the mane and tail, lower legs, and tips of the ears.

**Q** What's the difference between a pony and a horse?

**A** The most obvious difference is size, with ponies officially defined as equines that reach a maximum height of 14.2 hands measured at the withers. (See *Why are horses measured in hands, not feet?*, page 5.) Ponies are usually stockier than horses, with proportionally shorter

||||||||||||||||||||||||||||||||||||||||||||||||||||||||||||||||||||||||||||||||||||||||||||||||||||||||||||||

## Stars and Strips Forever

### FACIAL MARKINGS

**Badger face.** A black stripe or blaze on a white face; quite unusual.

**Baldface.** A very wide blaze that covers much of the face, including eyes and muzzle. Baldface horses often have blue eyes.

**Blaze.** A wide strip of white running down the length of the middle of the face.

**Snip.** A small strip or marking of white on the horse's muzzle between the nostrils.

**Star.** A white spot located between or above the eyes. Must be wider than a strip or blaze, if either is present.

**Strip.** A narrow line of white running down the middle and length of the face (also called a stripe or a race).

legs and thicker coats and manes. They are intelligent and dispro-portionately strong for their size. Many breeds originated in windy, storm-swept islands and cold, remote hill countries where animals with compact builds and sturdy constitutions adapted best to the lim-ited resources and harsh conditions. (See *What are some common pony breeds?*, page 103.)

> **FAST FACT** A small horse can be pint-sized without being a pony. Some small horse breeds, such as Falabellas and Caspians, have the conformation and proportions of a horse.

## Q Can you clone a horse?

A You can if you have upwards of $150,000. All you need to do is buy a kit from a gene bank and have your vet take a small tissue sam-ple (from the side of the neck or underneath the tail). The gene bank will take care of the rest. Sentimental (or greedy) owners should be

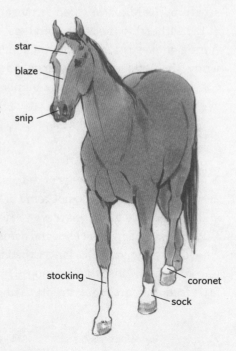

### LEG MARKINGS
**Coronet.** A narrow band of white hair around the coronet band at the top of the hoof, usually not wider than 1 inch (2.5 cm)

**Pastern.** White marking that extends from the top of the hoof, up to and as far back as the fetlock.

**Sock.** White marking that extends higher than the fetlock, but not halfway to the knee.

**Stocking.** White that goes from hoof to knee or higher.

star

blaze

snip

stocking

coronet

sock

aware, however, that although cloned animals have the same genetic makeup as the donor, certain physical characteristics and personality traits may be different because of the way genes are expressed.

The first cloned equid, a mule, was produced at the University of Idaho in 2003 (see *Cloned to Win*, page 152). A few weeks later, a cloned Haflinger horse was produced in Italy. Cloning continues today both in research laboratories and in private labs, but the cost has prevented the practice from becoming widespread. In addition, some registries, including the Jockey Club (Thoroughbreds) and the American Quarter Horse Association (AQHA), refuse to register cloned horses.

> FAST FACT: **To be registered, racing Thoroughbreds must be born as a result of "live cover," meaning that the stallion physically mates with the broodmare. Artificial insemination is not allowed.**

## Q What makes a donkey different from a horse?

A The donkey or ass (*E. asinus*) is a domesticated member of the horse family and a descendant of the African wild ass. They range in size from the Miniature Mediterranean type (under 36 inches/91 cm at the withers) to the Mammoth type (54–56 inches/137–142 cm). A male donkey is a jack, not a stallion, while a female is a jennet or jenny. Their offspring, however, is called a foal.

They differ from horses in a number of ways:

- ◆ Much longer ears
- ◆ Short, fuzzy, upright mane
- ◆ Tasseled tail
- ◆ Bray instead of neigh

Donkeys are usually gray or dun, but can be brown, black, roan, or even spotted, but they do not come in buckskin, pinto, or palomino, and they generally don't have white facial or leg markings. Many have a dorsal stripe down the back and across the withers.

Donkeys typically live longer than horses — 30 to 40 years is not uncommon. Because they developed in areas where there often was little feed, they are more capable than a horse of subsisting on fibrous

## THE EQUINE GENOME

The genome of an organism contains all of the biological information needed to build and maintain a living example of that organism. The biological information is encoded in molecular chains of deoxyribonucleic acid (DNA) and is divided into units called **genes**. A gene is the basic unit of heredity in a living organism, and the portion of DNA in each gene contains information that determine what the gene does. Sequencing or mapping the genome refers to determining the order of the components in a molecule of DNA.

The sequencing of the horse genome was completed and published in 2009 after more than 10 years of collaborative effort by an international team of scientists at 20 universities. The $15 million effort mapped the approximately 2.7 billion DNA base pairs in the horse genome, providing an invaluable tool for studying issues, including inherited diseases and disease-causing mutations, behavioral disorders, performance traits, and resistance and susceptibility to certain ailments.

plants. A donkey needs shelter from the rain because his coat can be penetrated by the water, unlike the denser coat of a horse.

Donkeys have small, box-like feet that often are so tough that shoes aren't required. They do, however, need regular trimming, just like a horse.

Donkeys are strong pack animals, able to carry over a quarter of their body weight. Evidence from skeletal remains indicates that humans have used them to carry loads since about 5000 BCE.

> *My favorite animal is the mule.*
> *He has more sense than a horse.*
> *He knows when to quit eating*
> *and when to quit working.*
>
> — HARRY S. TRUMAN

*This Poitou donkey is shown
with a miniature companion.*

# A Different Sort of Donkey

**THE RARE POITOU DONKEY,** developed in the Poitou region in
west-central France, became a symbol of distinction and prestige
among French noblemen during the Middle Ages. The salient
characteristic that distinguishes the Poitou from other donkeys is a
long, shaggy coat that can hang nearly to the ground in matted strips
of hair if not groomed.

   They are strong, sturdy animals, standing about 15 hands high, with
large, strong hooves. Because of their size, strength, and docility,
Poitou jacks were prized as sires of mules, especially when mated with
a breed of draft mares called Mulassier, a pairing that consistently
produced mules that were large, strong, and willing. As the demand
for draft mules declined around the world, so did the number of
Poitous. Fewer than 200 purebred Poitous exist today, with part-breds
numbering no more than 400.

## Q Where do mules come from?

A A mule is the hybrid offspring of a jack donkey and a female horse (a mare). Mating a stallion and a jenny, a much rarer pairing, produces a hinny. These offspring are almost always sterile because horses and asses have different numbers of chromosomes. Breeders use different-sized combinations of donkeys and horses to produce draft mules, riding mules, and mini mules.

Mules have a reputation for being stubborn, but in many cases, it is more a matter of the mule having more sense than its handler. When properly handled, mules are willing workers. They are usually

### THAT MULE IS A JUMPING FOOL

Mules can be as adept as horses in dressage, jumping, cutting, roping, barrel racing, and other events that require athletic ability. One event that is unique to mules, however, is jumping an obstacle from a standstill. The event has its roots in raccoon hunting in the mountains of the southern United States.

When a hunter, following the hounds on his mule, came to a wire fence, he dismounted and placed his jacket on the fence to provide the mule a clear look at how high he had to jump. The mule sat back on his haunches and performed a kangaroo-like leap over the fence. Most mule shows today include that type of jumping in the schedule of events; a wooden bar is used instead of a wire fence. Most mules can jump well over 5 feet and the world record is 8 feet.

stronger than horses, have more endurance, and consume less food. They are notoriously sure-footed on narrow mountain trails.

The mule has a strong survival instinct and rarely is willing to do something that might bring him harm. For example, many horses, if allowed unlimited access to grain, will gorge themselves until they become ill, while the mule, generally speaking, will eat only enough to satisfy his hunger.

> *The mule, he is a funny sight.*
> *He's made of ears and dynamite.*
> *He has a funny voice to sing*
> *And makes a noise like everything.*
> *Some folks don't treat mules with respect*
> *They say they have no intellect.*
> *The mule, he minds his own biz,*
> *He don't look loaded, but he is.*
>
> SUNG TO THE TUNE OF "MY MARYLAND" — author unknown

## Q Why don't you ever see anyone riding a zebra?

A A major difference between zebras and their equine cousins is personality. Zebras have never been fully domesticated and are only rarely tamed enough to be trained. They are said to be unpredictable, but have appeared in circus acts and other venues.

Zebras are a separate species (*E. zebra*) of the equine family with similarities to both horses and donkeys. (See *Are zebras equines?*, page 3; *Black and White and Black All Over*, facing page.) Zebras cannot run as fast as horses but, like horses, they will kick, rear, and bite when cornered by a predator. As are all equines, they are social animals, and their sensitive hearing and good eyesight equip them to be alert to predators and sensitive to one another.

> FAST FACT A donkey/zebra hybrid is called a zonkey, a zebroid, or a zedonk. A zorse, of course, is the offspring of a horse and a zebra.

*Lionel Walter Rothschild, the second Baron Rothschild, an English banker and animal collector, used zebras to pull his carriage through the London streets at the turn of the twentieth century.*

## BLACK AND WHITE AND BLACK ALL OVER

It is unlikely that large white animals would survive the major predators of the African habitat. Scientists believe that zebras are actually dark animals that developed white stripes as an adaptation to their environment, perhaps to help regulate heat absorption and/or to provide camouflage. Because the African tsetse fly prefers to bite large, dark animals, another theory suggests that the stripes offer zebras some protection from these vicious flies.

Zebras have black skin, except on their white bellies. The pigment of the stripes is in the dark hairs. The hairs in the white stripes have no pigment.

The patterns on each animal differ enough that researchers can identify individuals by their markings. The stripes might serve a similar social purpose for the animals themselves, providing visual cues by which they can identify one another. Stripe patterns also vary by subspecies; the markings of herds that are isolated from one another may therefore differ slightly.

## Q Walk, trot, canter — how do horses get where they're going?

**A** The walk, trot, and canter are the standard gaits done by most horses. Gaits describe the sequence of movements of a horse's legs.

*The walk is a four-beat gait with each foot striking the ground at a separate interval.*

*The trot is a two-beat gait with diagonal pairs striking the ground simultaneously — left front, right rear, and right front, left rear.*

*The canter is a three-beat gait with three feet in contact with the ground during each stride. At one point in each canter stride, the horse's weight is borne for a split second on one front leg.*

HORSE 101

**FAST FACT** When an excited horse refuses to walk quietly, but instead prances along with short little steps, it is called "jigging." Many riders discourage this gait because it can be uncomfortable to ride.

*When the horse increases speed and length of stride, the canter becomes a gallop. **The gallop** is a four-beat gait very much like the canter but faster, covering more ground.*

# Q What is a "gaited horse"?

A "Gaited" normally means that a horse moves his legs in such a way as to provide an exceptionally smooth and comfortable ride because at least one foot is on the ground at all times and there is no bouncing (unlike the trot). These gaits primarily appear as a natural trait in specific breeds, though training enhances them. Smooth gaits can range in speed from a rapid walk to a running step that rivals a full-out canter.

Examples are the **running walk** of Missouri Fox Trotters and Tennessee Walking Horses; the smooth movement of Paso Finos and Peruvian Pasos, whose short strides and rapid footfall translate into a ride that is smooth as glass; and the blazing fast **skeith tolt** (amble or stepping pace) of the Icelandic Horse. The **slow gait** and **rack**, both of which are four-beat gaits at varying rates of speed, are performed by Saddlebreds and normally reserved for the show ring. (See *Which breed is known as the "Peacock of the Show Ring"?*, page 90; *The Florida Cracker — Not a Snack*, page 98; *What is a Missouri Fox Trotter?*, page 99; *Are a Paso Fino and a Peruvian Paso the same breed?*, page 99; *Can Tennessee Walkers trot and canter?*, page 102; *What is a "Big Lick" Horse?*, page 186.)

# Q What's the difference between the right lead and the correct lead?

A At the canter (called the lope in Western riding), the horse starts each sequence of footfalls with one of his front feet (see illustration on page 16). That foot determines the lead. When traveling to the left in an arena, the horse is in best balance on the left lead and vice versa when he is going to the right; he is therefore on the correct lead, whether going to the right or to the left.

On the left lead, for example, the prime propelling force for each stride comes from the right rear leg, with the left front and left rear reaching forward in conjunction with the propulsion. The right front leg does not reach as far forward as the left front. A horse on the correct lead when traveling in a circle is in balance and well supported.

> **FAST FACT** Racehorses generally run on the left lead until they round the final turn and then switch to the right lead because the leading limbs have a tendency to tire first.

*When a horse canters on one lead in front and the other in back, as shown here, it is said to be "cross-cantering" or "cross-firing." A horse that canters in front while trotting behind may be called a "trashy loper."*

## CHANGING LEADS ON THE FLY

Horses on a jump course change leads as they change directions around the course. Being on the correct lead not only helps the horse balance properly in the ring, it is often part of judging in shows. In pleasure contests, horses are penalized if they don't pick up the correct lead when asked to lope or canter. Reining horses are penalized if they don't immediately switch leads when changing direction during a cloverleaf or figure-eight pattern.

In training, a horse is first taught to change leads by coming down to a trot and then picking up the opposite lead as it turns in the new direction. This is called a **simple change** of lead. Eventually, the number of trot strides asked for is reduced, and at a more advanced level, a horse learns to make a **flying change**, where it switches leads in mid-stride. Highly trained horses can make flying changes with every stride, so that they look as though they are skipping across the ring.

## Q What is a counter canter?

**A** A counter canter is when a horse is cantering on the opposite lead to the direction of travel. In other words, he is leading with his left front leg while moving around the ring to the right. This often happens when an inexperienced horse or rider doesn't understand the correct cues, but at higher levels of training, a counter canter is sometimes asked for on purpose. It can be used to physically condition the horse and to refine training.

## Q How far can a horse travel in an hour?

A Different breeds move with different strides, and conformation, age, and other factors influence their gait, but at the walk, most horses cover from 2 to 4 miles per hour (3–6 km/h). Horses in areas where grass is sparse might travel 10 miles (16 km) or more in a day as they meander and graze.

On average, a horse trots between 8 and 10 mph (13–16 km/h), and canters between 10 to 17 mph (16–27 km/h). The gallop depends on the horse's health, stamina, and breeding. An average gallop is 30 mph (48 km/h), but Thoroughbreds can reach 40 mph (64 km/h) and Quarter Horses have been clocked at 55 mph (89 km/h) as they crossed the finish line.

FAST FACT **It takes six strides and 2.5 seconds for a Thoroughbred racehorse to hit full speed.**

## Q How many horses are there in the United States? In the world?

A The horse population in the United States peaked at more than 20 million in about 1920, but as tractors, trucks, and automobiles took over the work formerly done by horses, that number declined drastically, going below 4 million by the early 1950s. Since then, interest in equine sports and pleasure riding has brought the total number of horses in the United States to nearly 10 million.

A 2006 report by the American Horse Council estimated the number of horses in the world at close to 60 million, while other estimates range up to 75 million.

FAST FACT **According to the American Donkey and Mule Association, there are about 150,000 donkeys in the United States, but the world population is estimated at over 44 million. The largest populations are in China, Pakistan, Ethiopia, and Mexico.**

## A MILLION OR MORE

The 2006 Global Horse Population report from the Food and Agriculture Organization of the United Nations found that there are more than 58 million horses in the world. The United States had the most — more than 9.5 million.

An American Horse Council report in 2006 listed nine other countries that had horse populations of over 1 million:

- ◆ China (7,402,450)
- ◆ Mexico (6,260,000)
- ◆ Brazil (5,787,249)
- ◆ Argentina (3,655,000)
- ◆ Colombia (2,533,621)
- ◆ Mongolia (2,029,100)
- ◆ Ethiopia (1,655,383)
- ◆ Russian Federation (1,319,358)
- ◆ Kazakhstan (1,163,500)

Two countries, Rwanda and St. Helena, reported no horses.

Among U. S. states, an American Horse Council report in 2005 found that Texas had the most horses with 978,822, followed by California (698,345) and Florida (500,124). The state reporting the fewest horses was Rhode Island (3,059), and the District of Columbia had only 33.

## Q What's the difference between a $1,000 horse and a $100,000 one?

A Whether bought at auction or in a private sale, purchasing a horse in North America can cost anywhere from a few hundred dollars to hundreds of thousands. The price is based on breed, bloodlines, age and health, training, and potential.

A stallion or mare with a distinguished pedigree and good breeding potential is worth more than a backyard gelding of indeterminate breeding. At annual stock sales in the racing world, yearlings with winning ancestors fetch high prices based on their earning potential. A horse with proven show experience or one that was trained by a respected trainer will fetch a higher price from people who compete at the top levels of dressage, jumping, reining, and other disciplines. Rare breeds or, in some cases, flashy coloring also command premium prices, but a sound riding horse of average quality normally will sell for somewhere between $2,000 and $3,000.

## Boom and Bust in the Arabian Market

THE ARABIAN BREED provides a classic example of how market forces can affect horse prices. Because of their beauty and mystique, Arabian horses became extremely popular during the '70s and early '80s, attracting attention from celebrities and high-profile businesspeople, who saw an equine investment as a potential tax writeoff. Breeders rushed to produce more foals and build palatial barns to house these equine treasures and attract wealthy buyers. Celebrities such as Bob Hope and the Pointer Sisters provided entertainment as part of extravagant auctions during which individual horses sold for a million dollars or more. At the apex of the boom in 1986, some 30,000 Arabian foals were registered.

The seeds of the inevitable bust were sown when Congress passed legislation that required horse owners to be actively involved with their horses before being able to deduct expenses against income from other sources. With this lucrative tax loophole closed, the market plummeted as investors by the hundreds left the business and demand for high-end Arabians disappeared. Soon, horses that had been selling for a million dollars were being offered for a few thousand dollars.

Breeding of mares dropped drastically; today, fewer than 7,000 Arabian foals are registered annually. With the market stabilized, talented, pedigreed Arabians can still sell for many thousands of dollars, but that demand is relatively limited compared with the unrealistic days of the '80s.

# Q Could a horse live in an average-size bedroom?

**A** A 10-by-12-foot (3m by 3.7m) bedroom is actually a bit bigger than most horses are used to. A horse kept indoors needs a stall that is large enough to move around and lie down in. A minimum of 80 square feet (7.4 m²) of floor space (an 8-by-10-foot [2.4 × 3.1 m] box stall) is recommended for the average 1,000-pound (454 kg) horse.

However, indoor life, even in a spacious stall, isn't good for horses at all. They need to move around to stay healthy and sound. A single horse needs an exercise area of at least a eighth of an acre (0.05 ha), preferably larger, and he needs from 1 to 3 acres (0.4 to 1.2 ha) to obtain adequate forage, depending on location. There is a big difference between the amount of grass available on an acre in the midwestern and southern states and an acre of land in the more arid Southwest.

Horses can survive nearly any extreme weather as long as they can escape from strong winds and penetrating rain. A fancy barn isn't required, but any horse kept outdoors should have access to a basic three-sided run-in shed. Barns must be well ventilated because stuffy, overheated living quarters can lead to respiratory disease. Horses usually prefer to be outside, even in inclement weather.

## THE PROBLEM OF UNWANTED HORSES

Owning a horse is a big responsibility, requiring a commitment of time, money, and emotional energy. A domestic horse can live for many years and relies completely on its owner, but changes in the economy or in the family can transform the joy of maintaining a horse into an unacceptable burden. There are always more horses available than the market can absorb, so selling an unwanted horse, especially one without good breeding, is often not an option.

Equine rescue and retirement facilities have limited capacity, and the cost of euthanasia and carcass disposal can put even that unpleasant option beyond reach. So, before you buy or breed a horse, it is responsible and humane to plan for the day when you may no longer be willing or able to provide its care.

Learn more at *www.unwantedhorsecoalition.org*.

# Q Do people still brand horses for identification? How is it done?

A Brand laws in the United States vary by region. Western states tend to have strict brand laws, while in most of the East and Midwest, brand laws are nonexistent. Where brand laws exist, breeders must have a new foal inspected by a brand inspector who issues a certificate declaring that person to be the owner, as proven by the dam's brand. If the branded horse is sold, a brand inspector checks the horse's brand against the brand shown on the certificate and issues the new owner "brand papers" that declare him or her to be the current owner. Whenever the horse is conveyed from the county or state of residence, the brand papers must accompany him.

**Hot-iron branding**, commonly seen in cowboy movies, is the traditional way that ranchers still identify their livestock. A branding iron marks the hide by stopping hair growth where the iron scorches the skin. The process results in a week or more of apparent pain and discomfort, with the branding site usually becoming swollen, warm, and sensitive to the touch.

**Freeze branding** uses extreme cold to kill the cells in the animal's skin that produce the hair color, resulting in white hair where the iron touches. The branding iron is cooled by a combination of dry ice, alcohol, acetone, and/or liquid nitrogen. The site is shaved before applying the iron, and in a few months, white hairs grow back in the shape of the brand. Advocates of freeze branding claim that the process is painless or nearly painless, causing only some puffiness that generally resolves in a few days.

**Hoof branding** is done by a farrier with a hot iron held painlessly against the hoof for about 18 seconds. It is used by horse traders when they do not need a permanent mark on the horse, and by others who prefer the ease of this method. Continual hoof growth means that the brand needs to be reapplied two or three times each year. States with brand laws normally require that brands be permanent.

FAST FACT Instead of brands, horses are sometimes identified with coded microchips placed beneath the skin. Racehorses are identified with lip tattoos.

Dutch Warmblood

Westphalen

*Some breed organizations have distinct brands that are applied as a sign of purebred status or acceptance of an individual as a breeding animal. Examples include the breeds shown here.*

American Trakehner

Haflinger

---

### HOOFING IT

Approximately 2,500 horses were used in the 1969 film *Undefeated*, starring John Wayne and Rock Hudson. This is believed to be the largest number of horses ever used in a film. The movie was filmed near Durango, Mexico, and the horses were leased from farmers and ranchers in the area. To make certain it would be returned to the proper owner, each horse had an identifying brand placed on one hoof.

---

## Q Do horses like to be petted?

A Horses are social animals and often rub their heads on each other or use their teeth to scratch each other's withers and the top of the croup, spots they can't reach themselves.

Just as with people, horses are sensitive to touch in various ways. Individuals react differently, but certain parts of the body are generally more sensitive than others. Thickness of hair and skin affects sensation, as does the personality of the horse. A calm, easygoing horse may accept patting that would irritate or upset a more nervous or energetic animal.

Generally speaking, horses seem to prefer being stroked or scratched rather than patted. A firm pat, while meant kindly, may feel more like a reprimand to the horse. Most horses like to be petted, however, and if you start out by rubbing him on his neck or back, he may eventually guide you to another spot that feels good to him.

*Social grooming is an important way that horses form bonds with each other. Within a herd, horses develop friendships and animosities, just as people do.*

### ALWAYS WEAR A HELMET!

Equine-related injuries account for over 100,000 emergency-room visits each year in the United States. Most of the injuries result from a fall while riding. Trauma to the head and neck is most common, followed by injuries to the arms and legs. It is estimated that more than 11,000 people annually experience traumatic brain injuries from horse-related incidents.

Less than 5 percent of reported horse-related injuries are from bites. An equine bite usually just results in a bruise or broken skin, but horses have sharp teeth and strong jaws that can cause more serious damage, like the loss of a finger.

CHAPTER TWO

# HOOVES, HEARING, AND HICCUPS

## Some Physical Facts

**n many ways,** horses are superbly adapted creatures, with their keen senses, instant reflexes, and incredible speed. In the wild, they thrive on grass and water, roaming for miles over rugged terrain and surviving harsh winters. For domestic animals, however, some of those adaptations can prove to be less than optimal. The equine digestive system is easily overloaded, sometimes causing serious and even fatal problems. Hooves that wear down naturally in the wild need to be trimmed regularly, with artificial shoes often taking the place of natural toughness. Slender legs can't always hold up to the stress of carrying a rider or competing rigorously. But for all their frailties, we still use the phrase "healthy as a horse."

# Q What does it mean to be "healthy as a horse"?

**A** A healthy horse has a good appetite and is alert and responsive. He has a shiny, sleek coat with no severe lumps or injuries. His eyes are bright and clear. Although he should not be bony or show ribs, being overweight is just as unhealthy for horses as it is for people.

A healthy horse turned out to pasture moves around a fair amount while grazing. He might play with his companions, buck, or gallop if feeling frisky. Horses usually snooze standing up, but lying down isn't necessarily a sign of ill health, as they often nap that way, sometimes stretching out flat on their sides.

# Q What does it mean for a horse to be "sound"?

**A** Soundness generally refers to a particular function, rather than overall health. A sick horse can be perfectly sound. On the other hand, a horse who is in generally good health can have a chronic condition that makes it unsound. Old-time horsemen utilized the term

## VITAL SIGNS

There's a broad range of "normal" for respiration, pulse and temperature, so horse owners should measure their horses several different times while at rest to form an idea of what is normal for each individual horse. It's important to know the baseline numbers so you can tell how different they are if the animal is stressed or ill. The following numbers are from the American Association of Equine Practioners.

- ◆ A relaxed horse breathes from 8 to 12 times per minute. Just count one rise and fall of the barrel (rib cage) as one breath.

- ◆ An adult horse's pulse should be between 32 and 36 beats per minute — you can take it with a stethoscope or by pressing two fingers against the large artery that runs under the horse's cheekbone.

- ◆ Normal rectal temperature is between 99.5 and 101°F (37.5 and 38.3°C). A thermometer used for a horse should have a string attached to it for safety, in case the thermometer slips into the rectum.

"sound" for horses that demonstrated no sign of lameness. A horse can also be "sound of wind," meaning it has no respiratory ailments, or "breeding sound," meaning that there are no impediments to a mare becoming pregnant and carrying a foal to term or for a stallion having the ability to impregnate a mare. In the lameness category, a horse might be guaranteed sound for Western or English pleasure classes, but not for eventing or jumping.

## Q Why do horses roll on the ground?

A Horses roll for a variety of reasons. A horse who is experiencing gastric trouble might roll to relieve abdominal pain (see *Colic: Not Just for Babies*, on page 36). More often, however, a horse rolls for a good scratch, perhaps after a sweat-inducing ride or training session. Rolling works dirt and dust into the coat, which may provide some protection against biting insects. A good roll also helps to stretch and strengthen the back muscles; a horse with a weak or painful back may be reluctant or unable to roll.

Some horses roll vigorously from one side to the other, while others stand up after one side and lie down again to reach the other side. Both ways are normal and may simply reflect a difference in conformation or conditioning.

*A healthy horse who lies down and rolls near other horses or when his owner or handler is nearby shows trust in his companions.*

*With good care and proper nutrition, a healthy horse can live well into his twenties or even thirties, even as he shows signs of aging, such as a swayback and hollowed eyes.*

## Q How do horses show their age?

**A** Like people, some horses age more quickly than others, depending on their genetics as well as on the environment in which they have lived and the nutrition and care they have received. In addition to generally slowing down and moving more stiffly, some signs of age in a horse include graying hair around the face, sagging muscles and weakened ligaments that result in a swayback, facial changes such as sunken eyes or boniness, and worn or missing teeth. (See *How long can a horse live?*, page 4.)

## Q Can an old horse be ridden?

**A** An older horse who is sound and in good health can still go for a gentle trail ride or make a wonderful mount for a child. Rides should be short with plenty of warm-up beforehand. An elderly horse with a swayback may become sore if ridden without proper precautions. A saddle that fits well is important, and a balanced, relatively lightweight rider maximizes the chances that a fit and experienced older horse will continue to be a sensitive and calm mount.

# Looking a Gift Horse in the Mouth

HORSES NEED TO BE ABLE TO CHEW FOOD PROPERLY to get all of their nutritional benefits, so healthy teeth are as important to a horse as they are to you. Dental problems can also affect a horse's attitude and his ability to respond to a bit in his mouth.

The front teeth or incisors are used for biting, and the back or cheek teeth grind down the fibrous food that makes up all or most of the equine diet. Unlike human teeth that stop growing once the permanent teeth erupt, a horse's teeth keep emerging for about 20 years. As the grinding motion of pulverizing food wears down the teeth, they keep growing to provide additional chewing surface. The teeth eventually wear down to a stub, and some may fall out.

Until a horse is 10 years old, examining the incisors can usually give you an idea of a his age. By the age of 5, a horse should have a full set of adult teeth above the gumline, with about 4 inches (10 cm) of tooth hidden in the jawbone. An experienced horse handler can guess the age of a horse under 5 years old based on which adult teeth are visible.

A young horse's adult teeth have dark indentations, called cups, in the center of each tooth. Looking at the lower incisors, you can observe that the cups gradually disappear as the surface of the tooth is worn down; by age 9 or 10 they are gone. After that, it is more difficult to estimate the age of a horse from his teeth.

*If a horse won't eat it, I don't want to play on it.*

— RICHIE ALLEN, former major league baseball player

## Q Will a horse eat a hamburger?

A Nature designed horses to survive on grass alone, but they often learn from humans that other foods can be tasty. Horses have been known to enjoy hamburgers and hot dogs, soda and beer, cookies and cupcakes, and all manner of fruits and vegetables. (See *Yes, We Do Eat Bananas*, page 42.)

Domestic horses are rarely turned out to graze all day as their sole source of nourishment, and in spite of their preferred snacks, most horses primarily eat hay, which is grass that is cured (dried) so that it can be stored without rotting. Hay for horses must be free of dust and mold spores; it loses nutritional value if not eaten within a year.

A normal horse can be perfectly healthy eating only good-quality hay, but horse owners have many choices from which to put together a healthy diet based on activity level, environment, general health, age, the weather, and special needs such as pregnancy, illness, or injury. For example, a horse who is worked extensively needs to eat more, and in cold weather, horses need more hay to keep their body temperature up. Grains or other concentrated foods can supplement forage if there is a need for weight gain, growth, increased milk production, or high levels of activity. Older horses may require a special diet if they have dental problems or other conditions that interfere with digestion.

*Horses are designed to graze continuously, rather than having one or two large meals a day. Turned out on good pasture, a horse may nibble for as many as 20 hours out of 24.*

# In One End and Out the Other

A HEALTHY 1,000-POUND (454 KG) HORSE produces about 50 pounds (23 kg) of manure each day. That amounts to **8 or 9 tons (1,000 kg) of manure per year per horse** to be mucked out of fields, pastures, and stalls and disposed of appropriately. In addition, the average horse produces from 6 to 10 gallons (22.7–37.9 L) of urine daily.

Manure management is a big issue for any horse keeper. Harmful parasite larvae can grow and feed on the nutrients in manure, and the combined wastes can provide ideal conditions for the growth of bacteria that are destructive to hooves. States and localities have differing rules about the distance permitted between manure piles and water sources or runoff areas, and owners of equine facilities may be required to file a waste management plan. Some horse owners find farmers who will take the waste to compost for fertilizer, but more and more owners must pay to have it hauled away.

Composting large amounts of manure requires careful management to avoid creating a fly-ridden, smelly, unusable pile. Successful composting kills parasites and pathogens, reduces the number of flies, and recycles the manure's organic matter and nutrients, making it a great way to fertilize pastures and gardens. (See *Minding the Manure*, page 230.)

## Q Can horses get stomachaches from eating too much?

A Horses are quite capable of doing just that. Turned out in a field, horses feed almost continuously, moving and grazing (called **trickle feeding**) for 16 to 20 hours a day. This natural way of eating keeps their stomach constantly busy with food passing through relatively quickly. Acids in the stomach begin breaking down the food, but horses are **hindgut fermenters**, meaning that most of the digestive process takes place in their long intestinal tract. (See *The Equine Digestive System*, page 35.)

Confined horses who are fed large amounts in just a couple of servings per day are most at risk for overeating. When food, especially grain, is available on an unlimited basis, a horse does not seem to be able to govern his intake and often will eat until he becomes ill. Horses can also make themselves sick on an overabundance of windfall fruit or if they don't drink enough water. (See *Colic: Not Just for Babies*, page 36 and *What is laminitis?*, page 52.)

FAST FACT **Unlike a horse, a mule will normally eat his fill and then stop before becoming ill.**

## Q Do horses ever have the hiccups?

A They do. With equine hiccups, the horse's abdomen contracts at the rate of 40 to 50 times per minute. Strenuous exercise, such as an endurance race, is usually the cause.

Exertion depletes electrolytes such as calcium, magnesium, potassium, sodium, and chloride, and when dehydration accompanies the hiccups, the condition can be serious and might require the attention of a veterinarian to reestablish a proper electrolyte balance. A solid conditioning program, proper nutrition, electrolyte supplementation, and plenty of water during exercise can usually prevent this problem.

FAST FACT **The medical term is "synchronous diaphragmatic flutter" (SDF), but old-time horse people refer to horse hiccups as "thumps."**

## Q Can horses vomit or burp?

A No, they cannot. The equine stomach is designed for frequent small meals. When a horse swallows food, it goes on a one-way trip through the digestive system; if he eats too much or eats food that makes him sick, he has no way to ease the discomfort. A strong, muscular, one-way valve (the cardiac sphincter) prevents the food from coming back up. (See *The Equine Digestive System*, facing page.)

Some gas naturally occurs in the stomach as part of the digestive process, and a large meal can cause a lot of discomfort. Because equines produce stomach acid constantly to digest frequent small meals, a horse's stomach functions best when it is about two-thirds full. An empty stomach can result in a buildup of stomach acids, and ulcers in the upper part of the stomach are common among domestic horses who go throughout the day without eating regular, small meals.

# The Equine Digestive System

**UNLIKE COWS AND SHEEP,** which are ruminants, horses have single-chambered stomachs. After food is chewed and swallowed, it moves through the 5-foot-long (1.5 m) esophagus to the stomach. Partially digested food then passes into the small intestine, which is about 70 feet (21 m) long. It takes anywhere from 30 to 90 minutes for the food to pass through the small intestine, where it is broken down into carbohydrates, fats, and proteins that are absorbed along with vitamins and minerals.

The next stop is the cecum, a pouch at the beginning of the large intestine where further digestion occurs before the food moves on to the large intestine. In the 12 feet (3.7 m) of the large intestine, fiber is broken down and the remaining nutrients are extracted. The whole process of feeding, digesting the nutrients, and expelling the waste products takes from 36 to 72 hours.

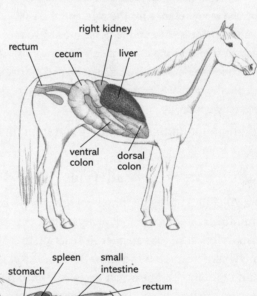

right kidney
rectum
cecum
liver
ventral colon
dorsal colon

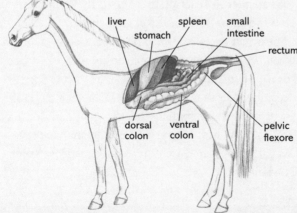

liver
stomach
spleen
small intestine
rectum
dorsal colon
ventral colon
pelvic flexore

# Colic: Not Just for Babies

COLIC IS NOT A SPECIFIC DISEASE but a general term for stomach pain or discomfort. Because horses are unable to vomit if they eat too much or ingest something poisonous, they are quite vulnerable to digestive upsets. When a horse develops colic, he may demonstrate discomfort by looking back or kicking at his sides, pawing, and lying down and rolling, as well as appearing to be depressed. The risks with colic are that a mass of food may cause a blockage, known as an impaction, in the gut or that repeated rolling may cause the intestines to twist, creating a dangerous and potentially fatal situation.

When a horse has colic, owners usually call a veterinarian because there can be many reasons for the pain and there is no simple cure-all. The classic treatment is to keep the horse moving to prevent the animal from rolling and to stimulate the elimination of feces or gas. A vet can relieve pain by injecting the horse with an analgesic and may administer fluids orally to try to get the digestive system working again. In serious cases, surgery may be the only option.

## Q Do horses have allergies?

A Allergies are signs of hypersensitivity — overreactions by the immune system to a food, drug, pollen, or insect bite. Hives are the usual clinical sign of an allergic reaction in a horse. They can develop anywhere from 15 minutes to 24 hours after exposure to the allergen, and typically disappear just as quickly with no serious consequences. Factors such as stress, heat, or pressure from the rider's weight in the saddle can cause or intensify an allergic response.

In rare instances, more serious complications can develop. Fluid may build up in the upper airway, making breathing difficult, or may occur in the eyelids, belly, or legs. A veterinarian may manage severe or chronic allergies with drugs such as epinephrine, corticosteroids, or certain antihistamines.

## Q Do horses need to take vitamins?

A Not unless their diet is lacking in some way. In almost all cases, horses receive the vitamins they need from their normal diet. Most horses do need access to a salt and/or mineral block as part of that balanced diet.

## Q How much water does a horse drink in a day?

A A normal horse drinks 5 to 10 gallons (19–38 L) of water a day, more in hot weather or after exercising. Many horses don't like very cold water and drink less in winter, which can lead to colic. Providing warm water is one way to ensure that they drink enough in cold weather.

---

### PICKY, PICKY

Some horses are quite fussy about their drinking water and refuse to drink unfamiliar-tasting water when away from home, particularly at horse shows or other events. Getting such a horse accustomed to a mild flavor, such as peppermint or molasses, in his water can help encourage him to drink when on the road. Packing a bottle of molasses is a lot easier than hauling a couple of days' worth of water from home.

---

## Q Do horses have good eyesight?

A Predators need sharp vision so they can locate prey from a distance and mount a sneak attack. Similarly, prey animals such as horses depend on spotting danger far enough away so that they can escape.

Hunters, such as lions, dogs, and humans, can usually see about 180 degrees by turning the head from left to right. Like the eyes of many predators, the human eye resembles an autofocus camera. It has powerful ciliary muscles that quickly focus on an object whether nearby or far away.

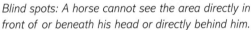

*Blind spots: A horse cannot see the area directly in front of or beneath his head or directly behind him.*

With his widely set eyes, a horse can see in a nearly complete circle when he moves his head from side to side. Although he can see almost all around himself, however, what he sees is not always accurate. He sees objects directly in front of him with both eyes (binocular vision), and objects on the side and toward the rear with one eye (monocular vision). Different parts of the brain receive images from each eye at the same time.

The eye of a horse is twice as large as that of a human, and it tends to magnify objects. The horse's ciliary muscles, however, do a relatively poor job of bringing objects into focus. A horse may be unable to identify an approaching object and will run away for a short distance, then turn and attempt to refocus by raising, lowering, or moving his head from side to side until the object comes into better focus.

> **FAST FACT** Equine eyes are the largest of any mammal; they are nearly twice as large as human eyes.

## Q Do horses see in color?

A Research suggests that horses have two-color (dichromatic) vision, so that reddish colors appear green. They can tell the difference between gray and either blue or yellow, but it is more difficult for them to see the difference between gray and green, and especially between gray and red.

## Q Can horses see in the dark?

**A** Compared with humans, horses have excellent night vision — about 50 percent better than ours. The pupil in a horse's eye is horizontal, allowing it to open or dilate quite widely, letting in a lot of light. The large cornea and retina give them a high level of sensitivity to light. In the wild, it is not unusual for them to graze at night and run in darkness over rough terrain.

> **FAST FACT** Horses have a good proprioception, which means they have a keen awareness of any movement in their body, allowing them to travel over rugged ground even in the dark.

## Q Do horses suffer from any eye problems?

**A** The prominently placed equine eye is vulnerable to any number of injuries and infections. Most horses have long eyelashes that protect the eye from dust and dirt. Like human eyelashes, they are sensitive to touch, setting off a protective blink reflex if something comes close.

A healthy eye is clear and bright, with the inside of the lid a pale pink. Eyes should be moist, and tearing should be minimal. A paler than normal eye membrane might mean the horse is anemic or it may have a digestive problem. If the eye is red, the horse may be feverish. Yellow membranes might indicate a liver problem, and bluish color may indicate heart or circulatory problems.

Horses are vulnerable to moon blindness, more correctly known as equine recurrent uveitis (ERU). This inflammation of the eyes waxes and wanes, hence the reference to the moon. Its cause is not completely understood, but it involves antibodies that mistakenly attack tissues in the eye. Horses and mules also get various malignant and benign tumors in the eye area, with some breeds and light-colored horses being predisposed to these problems.

A sex-linked, inherited form of blindness can occur in Thoroughbreds, Appaloosas, Paso Finos, and Standardbreds. Called congenital stationary night blindness, it causes poor night vision, although the horse has normal vision in daylight. It is "stationary" because it generally does not progress to impaired daytime vision.

# Violin Strings, Hair Shirts, and Diamonds: The Many Uses of Horsehair

IN THE NINETEENTH AND EARLY TWENTIETH CENTURIES, hair from the mane or tail was commonly woven into upholstery fabric and used as stuffing material for furniture. Early Christians used rough cloth made from animal hair as a means of bodily mortification and to help the wearer resist temptations of the flesh.

Today, horsehair is sold in different lengths and colors in 0.5-pound (0.2 kg) and 1-pound (0.5 kg) bundles. People use it as an extension to enhance a show-horse's tail, or for making violin bows, brushes, and jewelry. Hitching is a specific type of knotted work done with horsehair that may have originated in Spain. In the mid-nineteenth century, inmates sometimes did this work to pass the time in prison.

Some people commission jewelry or decorative pieces made as mementos from the hair of a favorite horse. A novel way to remember a favorite horse is to order a memorial diamond made of particles of carbon that are extracted from the hair of the deceased. The material is added to a diamond-growing foundation using a technique that involves high heat and high pressure over time (HHPT). It takes just over an ounce (35–40 g) of hair to produce a canary diamond and 3.5 ounces (100 g) for a blue diamond.

||||||||||||||||||||||||||||||||||||||||||||||||||||||||||||||||||||||||||||||||||||||||||||||||||||||||||

## Q How good is equine hearing?

A Horses have very mobile ears and generally acute hearing. The ears can rotate almost 180 degrees from front to back to focus on sounds. If you make a clicking or hissing sound without moving or giving any visual clue, a horse with normal hearing should react by looking toward you or pointing an ear in your direction.

Hearing declines with age, but before any hearing loss, horses can hear sounds between 55 and 25,000 hertz (Hz), with their best range between 1,000 and 16,000 Hz. They can sense the vibrations of very low tones even though they don't actually hear them with their ears.

*A horse's ears are always moving as he tunes in to his surroundings. The ears also give clues to the horse's state of mind. This one is listening to his rider while paying attention to something up ahead.*

Humans, in contrast, can hear best in the 1,000- to 4,000-Hz range. We can hear tones from as low as 20 Hz up to a high-pitched whistle of about 20,000 Hz.

## Q Can horses get rabies?

A The chances of a horse getting rabies are slim, but because the disease is 100 percent fatal in unvaccinated animals, it makes sense to inoculate against it. A few admittedly random statistics point out the rarity of rabies in horses: Only 52 horses have died of rabies in New York state since 1990. Of the 128 animals killed by rabies in Florida in 2007, only one was a horse. Of the 153,000 horses registered in Maryland in 2006, only two contracted the disease.

## Q Do horses catch colds?

A Horses catch colds just as people do and the treatment is much the same: plenty of rest, good nutrition, and ample water. Cold symptoms can include a depressed attitude, coughing, and mucus in the nostrils. Cold symptoms in the horse mimic those of more serious afflictions, such as equine flu or equine herpesvirus (EHV-4).

# Q Can people catch diseases from horses?

**A** Diseases that horses and other animals transmit to people are called **zoonotic diseases**. The saliva and nasal secretions of equines can transmit various bacteria, viruses, and parasites, either through direct contact with a person's skin or from inhaling respiratory droplets when a horse sneezes. Ringworm and other fungal skin diseases are contagious through skin-to-skin contact. Some forms of equine encephalomyelitis as well as acute equine respiratory syndrome caused by the Hendra virus can be serious and sometimes, though rarely, fatal when contracted by humans.

Some salmonella bacteria and protozoan intestinal parasites affect both horses and people, causing diarrhea and other complications. Transmission occurs from improper hand washing and other unsanitary practices when handling materials contaminated with infected feces.

---

### YES, WE DO EAT BANANAS

Scientists at the University of Southampton in England conducted an experiment to determine which flavors horses prefer. The purpose was to help design medicines and nutritional supplements that horses would be willing to eat, and indeed, the horses were much more willing to eat flavored mineral pellets than plain ones. Favorite flavors were fenugreek and banana. They also liked, in order of preference, cherry, rosemary, cumin, carrot, peppermint, and oregano.

---

# Q What kind of vaccinations do horses need?

**A** Vaccinations are one of several important ways to prevent diseases in horses. The type of vaccination required depends on where a horse lives, how he is used, whether he travels, and where and how likely he is to be exposed to other animals.

The vaccinations that every horse should normally have include tetanus, rabies, and Eastern and Western equine encephalitis. Veterinarians may also recommend specific vaccinations for horses in a particular region or against currently active diseases, just as a human flu vaccine is administered annually in response to currently active forms of the disease.

## Q How does a horse cool off in hot weather?

A Horses, like humans, have copious sweat glands and perspire all over their bodies to cool themselves. And as a horse's temperature increases, the bloodstream carries body heat to the skin's surface where perspiration forms and then evaporates, cooling the horse in the process. The veins of thin-skinned horses such as Arabians and Thoroughbreds often show prominently on the neck and shoulders in very hot weather or during heavy exertion.

## Cooling the Olympic Athlete

IN ANTICIPATION OF THE 1996 OLYMPICS in torrid Atlanta, Georgia, an ad hoc task force of veterinarians and horse industry representatives was set up to study the effects of heat and humidity on exercising horses, to avoid problems during the competitions. To help prevent horses from overheating, the task force recommended modifying the events by shortening the endurance test, reducing the number of jumps, and adding two rest periods.

The task force also developed a heat index for horses, inspired by the U.S. Marine Corps' heat index for humans. Taking into account heat, humidity, wind, and solar radiation, they were able to calculate the best time of day for the Olympic events. For example, the cross-country event in Atlanta began at 7 A.M. so that it was finished before noon.

Another discovery was that the initial layer of water from a hose quickly heats up and can prevent cooler water from reaching the skin, so the task force recommended the frequent use of a sweat scraper while hosing or sponging an overheated horse. Another recommendation was cooling out horses in front of fans if there was no breeze.

## Q How often does a horse need a bath?

**A** Many riders rinse sweat and dirt off their mounts after a vigorous ride. Show horses are accustomed to frequent shampoos as part of their competitive routine, but most domestic horses stay clean enough with regular grooming rather than a complete soaping up. Horses may need an occasional bath during warm weather, after a particularly good roll in the mud, or if a skin condition requires medicated shampoo.

It's important to clean a male horse's sheath (genital area) and a mare's udders periodically, but too many baths can dry out the skin. Thoroughly rinsing off all soap residue is critical, and in cold weather, the horse must be dried thoroughly before being turned out so that it doesn't become chilled. Many people put a conditioning cream in their horses' manes and tails after a bath.

*Regular baths aren't necessary for most horses, though many seem to enjoy being rinsed off with cool water after a vigorous ride. Some even learn to drink out of the hose.*

HOOVES, HEARING, AND HICCUPS

## Q How do horses stay warm in the winter?

A Most horses, left unblanketed during cold weather, will grow a thick coat of hair that traps warm air next to the skin. As long as they can find shelter from soaking rain and penetrating wind, horses readily survive harsh weather and below-freezing temperatures. In fact, horses will often stand outside in the rain or snow even if shelter is available.

Many owners prefer to blanket their horses during the winter, especially if they ride regularly. A horse with a heavy winter coat can become overheated, wet, and then chilled if worked hard. Older horses and ones with particular medical conditions may also require blanketing to keep warm in severe weather.

> FAST FACT A horse's thermal comfort range is estimated to be between 30 and 75°F (–1 to 24°C). This is the range within which he can maintain his body temperature without becoming overly stressed.

## Q What does it mean to float a horse's teeth?

A The constant sideways motion of chewing food often causes a horse's teeth to wear unevenly, eventually resulting in the formation of points and edges, called hooks, that inhibit proper chewing. If not attended to properly, this condition can eventually lead to malnutrition because food is not being thoroughly chewed.

*Regular dental attention is an important part of good health care for horses. This veterinarian is floating this horse's teeth, which means filing off the rough points that form over time as the horse chews.*

To produce a more even chewing surface and to remove hooks, the teeth are "floated," or filed down, with either a hand-operated or a power-driven file that grinds off the offending points and edges. Many veterinarians recommend examining a growing horse's teeth every six months, with annual exams for adult horses.

---

## HOW MUCH BLOOD?

The average 1,000-pound (454 kg) horse contains about 9 gallons (34 L) of blood, but the amount varies according to breed. The volume of blood can have a significant bearing on the horse's ability to perform at a high level, such as racing, so it's not surprising that Thoroughbreds have the most blood in relation to body weight compared to other light horses. Draft horses, in spite of their size, have the least.

---

## Q Do horses breathe through their mouths?

A Horses can't breathe through their mouths as do many other animals, but nature has compensated by providing large nostrils that expand when more oxygen is needed.

## Q What are windpuffs and thoroughpins?

A **Windpuffs** are fluid-filled swellings in the back of the fetlock joints in front or rear limbs. The condition usually doesn't require treatment unless the horse is lame, in which case it can be a warning sign that something is amiss. Windpuffs are most often found in young horses in training and they disappear as the horse becomes more fit.

A **thoroughpin** is a puffy, small swelling at the side of the hock. Like a windpuff, it is not usually a serious condition.

## Q Why do horses have to wear shoes?

A In the wild, horses roam over miles of rocky ground, and their hooves pretty much trim themselves. With natural selection weeding out poor hooves, wild horses generally have very tough feet that are suited for rough going.

As tough as their hooves appear, domestic horses often need extra protection from the wear and tear caused by riding, walking on hard surfaces, jumping, racing, and other activities. The outside wall of the hoof can chip and crack, while the bottom of the foot can be bruised or overstressed. Poor nutrition and genetics can also affect hoof strength and soundness.

Hooves, like human fingernails, grow continuously and need regular trimming, even if the horse is not shod. Overgrown hooves are more prone to damage and can interfere with the gaits. As a rule of thumb, a farrier should check the horse's hooves at least every eight weeks, which means pulling the shoes, trimming the hoof and resetting the shoes.

## Q What's a barefoot horse?

A Many domestic horses with strong, healthy hooves can go without shoes, depending on the amount of riding or work they do and on what type of terrain. A variety of styles of hoof boots are available for use on long rides or rough ground.

FAST FACT **Using some sort of covering to protect hooves is ancient history, starting with rawhide or leather wraps. The first evidence of iron horseshoes comes from the fifth century.**

*Blacksmiths used to forge individual shoes, a process known as "hot shoeing." Today, while hot shoeing is still practiced, many farriers prefer to "cold shoe," using premade horseshoes. These come in several sizes and can be nailed directly to the hoof.*

# Q Does it hurt a horse to have its hooves trimmed?

A No more than it does to clip our toenails. Inside the hoof wall, however, is a layer of nerves and blood vessels, and if the hoof is trimmed too short or a nail is improperly driven and contact is made with the sensitive interior, the horse will feel intense pain, much as a person would if the fingertip were nicked. In addition to being painful, penetrating this sensitive area can open the door for harmful bacteria.

# Q How fast do a horse's hooves grow?

A On average, a horse's hoof grows from 0.25 to 0.38 inch (0.6–1 cm) per month. The growth occurs from the coronary band down. (The coronary band is at the very top of the hoof and contains myriad blood vessels that supply the foot with nourishment. A healthy coronary band correlates to a healthy hoof. If the coronary band is damaged, the growth pattern of the hoof is disturbed and the result might be a misshapen hoof.) The average hoof is 3 to 4 inches (7.6–10.2 cm) long, so the horse grows an entire new hoof each year.

Factors such as nutrition and exercise, as well as the type of ground the horse is kept on, can affect hoof growth. Nutrition level is another factor. The correct amount of nutrients stimulates more rapid hoof growth.

FAST FACT **Hooves grow fastest in spring and slowest in winter. Rear hooves typically grow faster than front hooves.**

## A QUESTION OF BLACK AND WHITE

In spite of the persistent myth that black hooves are stronger than white ones, research shows no difference in hoof strength or durability based on color. A variety of other factors, including genes and too much or too little moisture, do affect hoof health. Nevertheless, many horse people swear by the old adage:

One white foot — buy him.
Two white feet — try him.
Three white feet — look well about him.
Four white feet — go without him.

# Q Why is there a frog on the bottom of the hoof?

**A** The frog is the V-shaped pad at the bottom center of a horse' foot. Its prime function is to absorb concussion. When a horse puts weight on the foot, the frog comes into contact with the ground and compresses. In doing so, it transmits pressure to the elastic structures of the foot. This, in turn, aids in blood circulation, absorbs concussion, and provides grip with the ground surface. If the frog does not transmit pressure to the elastic structures of the foot, there is danger that the hoof will shrink inward, with the result being contracted feet and lameness.

> **FAST FACT The grooves on each side of the frog are called "commissures," but no one seems to know why the frog is called a frog.**

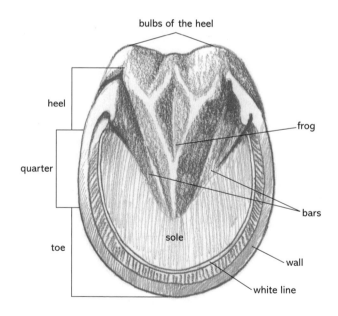

bulbs of the heel

heel

quarter

toe

frog

bars

sole

wall

white line

# Conformation Problems

**WHEN A HORSE'S LEGS ARE IMPROPERLY FORMED,** he often is unable to perform at an optimum level, and the condition might be the precursor of lameness from undue stress on muscles and joints. Here are some common conformation faults of the legs:

❮ **Base-narrow (bow-legged).** The distance between the hocks is greater than the distance between the back feet. This is a more severe condition than base-wide because of the extra stress placed on the entire hock joint with each step.

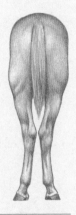

❯ **Base-wide (cow-hocked).** The distance between the hocks is less than the distance between the feet. Unless the condition is severe, it might not impede a horse's performance, but as it often places undue stress on the hocks, it could lead to lameness problems.

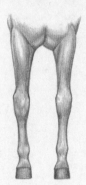

❮ **Bow legs.** The distance between the knees is wider than the distance between the feet, putting undue stress on the joint and creating a weak leg.

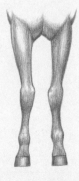

❯ **Knock knees.** The distance between the knees is less than the distance between the feet; this is not as serious a conformation flaw as bow legs.

**‹ Camped in (sickle-hocked).** When we look at a well-conformed horse from the side, an imaginary plumb line can travel vertically along the rear of the cannon bone between the hock and fetlock, hitting the ground behind the rear hoof. With the sickle-hocked horse, there will be space between the plumb line and the rear cannon bone, from the upper point of the hock downward.

**› Camped out.** The opposite of sickle-hocked. The rear legs extend to the rear from the hocks down, cutting down on impulsion from them.

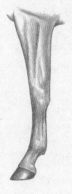

**‹ Behind at the knee (calf knee).** Instead of the leg being straight from top to bottom, the horse's knees are set behind an imaginary straight line. This undesirable conformation allows the knee to hyperextend or bend backwards, which can place a great deal of stress on ligaments and tendons as well as on the knee joint itself.

**› Over at the knee (buck knee).** The opposite of calf knee. When viewed from the side, the knee is forward of the connecting leg bones. The fault is not quite as serious as calf knee because it often results in less stress on the joint.

## Q What is "overreaching"?

A When a horse walks, the rear hoof lands in the impression made by the corresponding front foot. This is considered a normal stride. Some horses, either because of poor conformation or faulty shoeing, reach farther forward with the rear leg (overreach) and might strike the front foot before it is out of the way. This is also known as "forging."

In severe cases, a front shoe might be torn off or the horse might injure itself by striking the front fetlock with the toe of the back foot. In many cases, corrective trimming and shoeing can solve the problem. When it can't, protective boots can be placed over the front feet and ankles.

## Q What are chestnuts and ergots?

A **Chestnuts** appear above the knee on the inside of the front legs of a horse and below the hock on the inside of the rear legs. They can be large or quite small. The rough texture is a bit like the hoof in that the surface can be pared or clipped off without causing the horse pain. **Ergots** are much smaller and are located at the back of the fetlock on all four legs. They normally are covered with hair and not visible.

A number of scientists believe that chestnuts and ergots are the remnants of the pads that were under the toes of the early ancestor of the horse. They hold that about 50 million years ago, the first known ancestor of the horse, *Eophippus*, had four padded toes on the front legs and three padded toes on the rear.

## Q What is laminitis?

A Laminitis, often referred to as founder, is inflammation of the sensitive inner structure of the foot within the hoof wall. The causes are many and varied and could include eating too much grain or lush grass, being ridden at a fast pace on a hard surface, infection, or foaling problems.

Laminitis can strike all four feet, but it is more common in the front feet. The afflicted horse is in intense pain and typically will rock back on his rear legs to alleviate weight and pressure on the front feet. If left untreated, the condition can cause serious and lasting damage to the foot.

## Q Is it dangerous to ride a horse on pavement?

A It can be dangerous, especially if the horse has shoes. Without shoes, the bottom of the foot allows the horse to obtain some purchase, but iron shoes on hard pavement provide little grip and have the potential for slipping. Most horses would prefer not to travel on pavement anyway because of the uncertain footing and because the unyielding surface is uncomfortable for their feet.

It is particularly dangerous to gallop a horse on pavement, not only because of the potential for a fall, but also because the concussion is beyond what the horse's shock-absorbing mechanism in his feet, ankles, knees, and legs can handle. Laminitis (see previous question) is one potential consequence, as is soft tissue damage that may take a long while to heal.

Police and carriage horses who routinely spend their time on city streets are fitted with special shoes. Some of them feature rubber soles that provide grip and help absorb concussion.

Interestingly, riding on ground that is too soft or yielding can also be detrimental. Unstable sand, deep snow or mud, overly thick arena footing, and slick grass can create undue strain on muscles and ligaments or can cause a horse to stumble or slip, possibly injuring himself.

## FOR WANT OF A NAIL . . .

*For want of a nail, the shoe was lost;*
*For want of a shoe, the horse was lost;*
*For want of a horse, the rider was lost;*
*For want of a rider, the battle was lost;*
*For want of a battle, the kingdom was lost,*
*And all for the want of a horseshoe nail.*

This little poem shows how important proper shoeing can be. It's unknown who invented the first horseshoes, but historical evidence shows that leather booties were used by early Asian and Roman riders. Metal horseshoes were in use in Europe by the fifth century.

Many people today are advocates of horses going barefoot or without shoes. Proving that what goes around, comes around, some riders use leather boots to protect hooves when riding on hard or rocky ground, but leave the hoof bare otherwise.

## Q Why do foals have such long legs?

A As a prey animal, horses need to be alert and mobile very soon after being born. A foal needs those gangly legs so he can reach his mother's udder and so he can keep up with her when the herd moves. A healthy foal should be on his feet and nursing between 30 minutes and an hour after birth.

FAST FACT The average gestation period for a horse is 336 days, but it can vary from 310 days to as many as 370 days.

*Foals are usually weaned around 4 months of age, but in the wild, a mare will allow the foal to nurse until shortly before she gives birth again. If the mare does not become pregnant again, she might allow the foal to nurse until it is 2 years old, although there is very little nutritive value in the milk by then.*

## UNIVERSAL BIRTHDAY

All horses officially become one year older on January 1. The universal birth date was established to simplify age requirements for racing and horse shows. As a result, many breeders attempt to have foals born as soon after January 1 as possible because a horse born on January 2, for example, will be far more developed when he reaches his first birthday than one born on June 1 of the same year. The advanced development can have a significant bearing on prices paid at yearling auctions, especially Thoroughbred sales, as well as on the horse's ability to perform against his peers at 2 and 3 years old.

# CHAPTER THREE

# HORSING AROUND

## Exploring Equine Behavior

Despite centuries of domestication, the horse is still driven by its evolution as both a creature of prey and a social being. In order to understand our equine companions and work with their nature, not against it, we must understand the instincts of a prey animal, with its keen senses and its "flight or fight" response to fearful situations. But it is the social nature of the horse, with its highly developed ability to communicate and to form bonds, that allows the wonderful partnership between human and horse to exist.

# Q Do horses have friends?

A Although long domesticated, horses are not suited for living alone. They are social animals and do best with company. Many horses form close bonds with stable or pasture mates and may object to leaving them behind when their owners come for a ride. If there are no other horses around, they like to have a donkey, goat, or other animal for company (see *Companion Animals*, below).

In the wild, horses live in small bands with complex relationships and interactions. Equine society is roughly hierarchical, with more dominant individuals establishing their position and determining access to resources. Less dominant members of a herd sometimes challenge authority, and the social order may change as the composition of the herd changes. (See *Home, Home on the Range*, page 197.)

FAST FACT **A horse that whinnies for its friends, resists leaving them behind, and tries to return to the barn rather than paying attention to its rider is said to be "herd-bound" or "buddy sour."**

## COMPANION ANIMALS

As animals who evolved to live in herds with strong social connections and complex interactions, horses do not do well in solitary confinement. Although a single horse may live contentedly enough in some cases, others develop behavioral issues or vices (see *The Vice Squad*, page 70). Others may act inappropriately with humans, becoming pushy and seeking attention.

Although probably happiest with another horse for company, horses have a remarkable ability to form strong bonds with other animals. Tales abound of lasting friendships between horses and donkeys, goats, cows, dogs, even cats. Many racehorses have a barn pal to help keep them calm and relaxed when they are not racing, and breeding stallions, who are often kept isolated from other horses, benefit from a non-equine companion.

The phrase "to get your goat" is said to come from the practice of racing stables' stealing the companions of rival racehorses in order to upset them before a big race.

## Q Are horses naturally monogamous or polygamous?

**A** They definitely are polygamous. In the wild, a stallion typically gathers a harem of mares and fights off other stallions during the breeding season so that he can mate with all of them. Mares remain with the stallion as long as he is in command. If another male drives him off, the mares will become part of the new stallion's harem. (See *Home, Home on the Range*, page 197.)

## Q How do horses defend themselves?

**A** The fight/flight response is the natural choice of defenses available to all animals. As prey animals, horses have keen eyesight and acute hearing to alert them to danger, and they instinctively flee when they feel threatened, rather than responding aggressively by attacking or facing off against the source of danger. When a horse is unable to flee, however, he will resort to the use of hooves and teeth as defensive weapons. He might bite, strike out with his front feet, or deliver vicious kicks with his rear feet. (See *Are horses ever aggressive?*, page 65.)

*While horses would almost always rather run than fight, they are quite capable of defending themselves and can inflict serious, even fatal, wounds with their hooves and teeth.*

## Q Why do horses buck and rear?

A Bucking and rearing are primarily defensive maneuvers that horses employ when running away isn't an option. Bucking, in particular, probably arises from a primal instinct to escape predators that drop from overhanging branches. Rearing allows a horse to strike out with his forelegs to fend off an attacker. Stallions also rear when fighting, and horses sometimes rear while playing.

Although a well-trained horse rarely bucks or rears, some horses do habitually try to unseat their riders. While such dangerous behaviors can usually be traced to poor training, both responses can have other causes. A sore back, improperly fitted saddle, or badly balanced rider can cause so much discomfort that a horse will buck.

A horse might rear in an effort to avoid the pain of an improperly fitted bit or a heavy-handed rider. Another cause of rearing may be when a horse is urged to move forward while being held back, giving him nowhere to go but up.

## Q What's the difference between neighing and nickering?

A Neighing or whinnying is a loud, long-distance greeting to another horse or to a person with whom they have a favorable association. Horses often whinny to one another when being separated or reunited, as when one is ridden away from the stable, leaving a buddy behind. Neighing can also serve as a warning or to solicit attention. Nickering is a quieter, close-up greeting, used by a mare with her foal or to greet a favorite human (often heard at feeding time).

**FAST FACT** A neighing horse can be heard as far as half a mile (0.8 km) away.

## Q Do horses sneeze?

A Horses cough, but they don't sneeze. If a horse gets something up his nose, he attempts to dislodge it with a long blast of air, often accompanied by lowering or shaking the head, which differs somewhat from the snort described on page 63.

# Horse Talk: How Horses Communicate

AS DO ALL SOCIAL CREATURES, horses communicate in a variety of ways. They are certainly great communicators at feeding time — nickering, pawing, and moving about the stall when they hear the rattle of feed buckets.

Horses employ numerous distinct vocalizations, and being highly visual animals, their body language clearly indicates feelings and intentions. For example, when two stablemates are reunited after being separated, they may **nicker** softly, and **nuzzle** and sniff each other with **ears pricked forward.**

When horses meet, they may **stand nose to nose** and blow into each other's nostrils to exchange scents and evaluate their relationship to one another. When two strange horses meet, they might **put their ears back and lower their heads.** As they sniff each other, one or both might **stamp a foot** or **squeal** as they establish who's who. They may also **move stiffly,** expressing tension or apprehension.

Horses primarily communicate with posture, position, and movement. The way a horse stands can tell his herdmates to be on alert or to relax and graze. **Head up and ears pricked** indicate that something's up. A **hunched shoulder or haunches** turned toward another horse (or human) means "stay away" or "watch out."

A **gentle licking or chewing motion** is understood as "I'm not threatening you." Horse trainers look for that signal to indicate that a horse is thinking about and accepting the current lesson.

## HORSE BODY LANGUAGE

THREATENING

ALERT

RELAXED

## NOW EAR THIS!

A horse's ears can tell a great deal, indicating, among other things, aggression, warning, attention, or calmness.

When a horse puts his **ears forward**, for example, it usually means he is curious, paying attention, or feeling friendly (A).

**A.** CURIOUS

While being ridden or driven, he will often turn **one ear backward** to concentrate on what the handler wants, and point the other one forward to be alert to his surroundings (B).

**B.** ATTENTIVE

A horse with **extremely pricked ears**, wide eyes, and head held high is frightened or worried (C).

**C.** FEARFUL/WORRIED

Both **ears turned backward** in a relaxed manner indicate that the horse feels safe. A bored or sleeping horse may let his **ears flop** almost to his neck (D).

**D.** RELAXED

A horse with **ears pinned back** and folded flat to his neck may be afraid or annoyed, but this threatening gesture clearly says *stay away* (E).

**E.** ANGRY

(continued)

## Horse Talk (continued)

### TELLING TAILS

The tail is another important part of equine communication. When a horse **flicks or wrings** his tail from side to side, especially when being ridden, it is a strong indication that he is unhappy, uncomfortable, or both. In horse-to-horse communication, a **tail held to one side** by a female indicates she is receptive to mating.

With all horses, an **upraised or flagged tail** is an indication of excitement. When horses escape confinement, for example, they often will dash about excitedly with their tails in the air. The opposite, a **tail clamped tightly** to the haunches, shows nervousness, tension, or anxiety.

*This horse is clearly excited about something — he may have just been turned out after a night indoors or he may have spotted another horse coming up the road.*

## Q Do mares have special ways to "talk" to their foals?

A Mares have several calls for their foals, ranging from a soft nicker when both are quiet and content to a high-pitched, anxious whinny when they are separated. When a young foal is still nursing, the dam will nicker softly and use her nose to help guide him to the food source.

As the foal matures, he might become overly enthusiastic while nursing and the mare will reprimand him with bared teeth and pinned ears or even a quick nip. As the foal becomes more adventurous, he might wander away while exploring his new world. The mare may seek to call him back, even trotting after the youngster, nickering urgently.

> FAST FACT **Foals indicate their status to other horses by gently "snapping" or "clacking" their jaws in a signal of submission.**

## Q Why do horses snort?

A A soft snort or deep sigh often indicates that the horse is relaxed or content. A deep, sharp exhalation through the nose with the mouth closed and head raised, however, usually signifies alarm or warns of potential danger. A snort like that given on a trail ride should alert the rider that her horse is frightened and might be looking for an escape route.

## Q What do horses use their tails for other than swishing away flies?

A Some scientists believe that early in the evolutionary process, the horse's tail was used to help propel the horse's body along, similar to the tails of some dinosaurs. As the horse developed legs that could carry him at a swift pace, however, there was no need for a tail to help with propulsion. Today, horses use the tail as a means of communication (see *Horse Talk*, pages 60–62) and also as something of a balancing device when running. In addition, it protects the female genitalia.

## Q What is a "fly frenzy?"

**A** All animals hate biting pests, but horses can become so frantic to escape these tormentors that they gallop around frantically, sometimes injuring themselves or becoming dangerously dehydrated in hot weather. Different species of flies attack different parts of the horse's body.

**Face flies** feed on mucus secretions from the eyes and nose.

**Stable flies** feed on blood, usually drawn from the legs and belly. Stable flies normally feed outdoors, so it is important that horses have a cool, dark place in which to escape.

**Blackflies** feed on blood from inside a horse's ear. They may be so abundant that they are drawn into the horse's air passages.

**Horseflies** take blood from the upper body, and their bites are quite painful. Blood loss can be significant, and one study estimated that a horsefly consumes 1 cubic centimeter (cc) of blood for a meal.

FAST FACT **Twenty or 30 horseflies feeding on a horse could drain 20 teaspoons of blood in 6 hours or a whole quart in 10 days.**

*A mesh fly mask protects against annoying biting insects while still allowing the horse to see. Some people put fly sheets over the horse's body as well.*

## Q Which has a better memory, a horse or an elephant?

**A** Like the celebrated elephant, horses have excellent memories, which makes them extremely trainable. If an experience is reinforced with positive training, they can learn a variety of behaviors and will anticipate what is wanted from them. They also accumulate bad memories and, like people, they can be traumatized by harsh treatment and will not easily outgrow a fearful reaction. For example, a horse who has been severely whipped may later sweat, roll his eyes, and try to escape when he simply sees a whip.

## Q How does a horse show pain?

A It depends on where the pain is located. A horse with a severe stomachache might move around restlessly or lie down and roll. He might bite at his side or kick at it with a rear foot. If a horse has an injured foot or leg, he will limp and might hold the painful limb off the ground. Quite often when horses are in pain, they are listless and don't eat as much as usual.

## Q Are horses ever aggressive?

A Wild stallions exhibit aggressive behavior when they are competing for access to a mare. Sometimes they merely posture with loud squeals and stamping front feet, but their behavior can escalate into full-blown conflict. In domestic settings, some horses, both male and female, are aggressive by nature, although in many cases, their behavior stems from fear or mistrust in response to mistreatment by humans.

Some horses are just plain mean, however. A naturally aggressive horse appears to set up an invisible barrier, and other horses and even humans who violate the barrier are in danger of being attacked. The attack could be a threatening move toward the violator, or it might involve an actual bite or a kick. Such a horse is fiercely protective of his space and usually will remain that way for life. (See *How do horses defend themselves?*, page 58.)

## Q Why do horses sleep standing up?

A Most typically, you see a horse dozing upright because sleeping on his feet allows him to be ready for instant flight should a predator approach. Horses have a **stay apparatus** that allows them to lock their limbs in place and expend little energy to remain standing while they rest or sleep lightly. The front legs rest in a straight position that holds most of their weight, and they can cock one hind leg into a resting position. A snoozing horse stands with head hanging low, and eyelids and lower lip relaxed and drooping.

Horses do sleep lying down for short periods, in either a recumbent or prone position. When simply resting, they generally are recumbent, which means they fold their legs beneath them and rest on their chest. On a sunny day and when feeling safe, they will be more apt to stretch out in a prone position, lying flat on one side with head and neck extended.

|| FAST FACT **Horses sleep in short stretches for a total**
|| **of 5 to 7 hours a day.**

## Equine Intelligence — How Smart Is a Horse?

**FOR MANY YEARS,** researchers have placed the horse near the bottom of the list in animal intellect, with apes, whales, pigs, dogs, elephants, cats, and even squirrels ranking higher. More recent research, however, is challenging the notion that horses aren't as intelligent as other animals. Evelyn Hanggi of Equine Research Foundation in California says that although many horse people still believe that horses have a limited capability to learn, she and her staff have discovered through research that the opposite is true. According to Hanggi,

> In reality, horses manage not only ordinary daily cognitive tasks, but mental challenges as well. In the wild, they must cope with food and water of inconsistent quality or unpredictable distribution, predators who change locations and habits, and a social system in which identities and roles of individuals must be discovered and remembered.
>
> Domesticated horses may face even more potentially bewildering conditions. In addition to dealing with similar situations encountered in nature, many domesticated horses must live in largely unsuitable environments, must suppress instincts while learning tasks that are not natural behaviors, and must coexist with humans who sometimes behave bizarrely, at least likely from an equine standpoint. Horses, both feral and domesticated, are faced with various conditions that require an assortment of learning and perceptual capabilities.

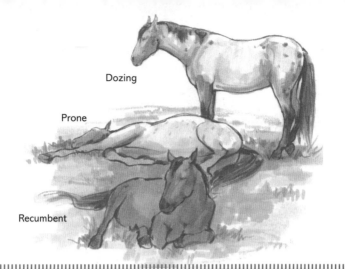

Dozing

Prone

Recumbent

## PLAYING WITH TOYS

Many animals thought of as intelligent (dolphins, wolves, chimpanzees) demonstrate playful behavior that seems to serve no discernable purpose. Similarly, many horses not only play physically with one another, but seem to enjoy playing with objects. Sometimes in a pasture setting, a horse will pick up a stick and toss it about or carry it around in his mouth, just as a dog might. Others will pick up an object such as a rubber feed pan and toss it through the air.

Providing toys to a horse who spends a lot of time in a stall can prevent boredom that can lead to destructive behavior, such as pawing or kicking at walls. (See *The Vice Squad*, page 70.)

*Horses enjoy batting at objects hanging from the ceiling, pushing a large rubber ball around, or carrying and tossing toys with handles.*

## Q Do horses yawn when they're tired?

A There seem to be many explanations for why horses yawn, but it's not because they're sleepy. Some horse trainers believe that horses yawn after being tense or working hard, because they have been holding their breath and are trying to replenish oxygen reserves, but as horses can't breathe through their mouths, this doesn't seem likely.

Horses often yawn after their bridles are removed (and some yawn when they see the bridle coming), which might indicate a need to stretch their jaws after (or before) working in a noseband and bit. But many horses yawn during acupuncture, massage, or chiropractic sessions, indicating that it is a sign of relaxation, not tension.

It's possible that yawning could be an effort to ease a toothache or stomach pain, so an unusual number of yawns warrants closer attention. But mostly, horses just seem to yawn when they feel like it.

## Q Why do horses paw the ground?

A One way horses explore their environment is with their hooves. Pawing can express anticipation, impatience, nervousness, or fear. It could also indicate that the horse is in pain. A horse may paw at the ground to judge its softness or solidity, such as before lying down to roll, or may examine an unfamiliar object with a hoof as well as with his mouth. Horses paw at water to gauge its depth or perhaps to stir it up before they drink. Especially in the wild, horses may paw to uncover dry grass under the snow or to dig up roots during a dry season.

From a horse in a stall, pawing may signal that a horse wants food or water or that he is bored. He may paw or even bang a foot on the stall door in anticipation, knowing that food is on its way. For some horses who are confined and lack exercise, pawing can become an ingrained and destructive form of repetitive behavior similar to cribbing. Like any vice (see *The Vice Squad*, on the next page), it may eventually injure the horse, and it can cause a shoe to loosen or pull off. Plenty of exercise and time to graze is helpful in preventing the behavior from becoming a problem.

## Q What's a horse laugh?

A The definition of "horse laugh" is "loud, coarse laughter" that resembles whinnying. Horses may have a sense of humor, but they aren't known for chuckling or guffawing. Sometimes, though, horses do throw up their heads and pull back their lips in an expression that can look quite humorous.

When a horse curls his upper lip back against his nose, he is exhibiting the **flehmen response**, which exposes the vomeronasal organ (also known as the Jacobson's organ) located in the roof of the mouth just behind the incisors. The organ absorbs pheromones — scented molecules — and transfers the information to the brain.

The flehmen response is most frequently observed when sexual behavior is involved, as when a stallion scents a mare in estrus. Although most frequently observed in stallions, it also occurs in mares, geldings, and foals in response to smells that are unusual or unpleasantly strong.

*The flehmen response is exhibited by other mammals (cats, for example) that also have a vomeronasal organ.*

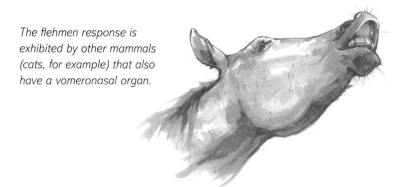

# Q Do a horse's eyes say anything about his personality?

A A horse's eyes are indeed a mirror of his soul, so to speak. Just as is the case with humans, equine personality can be guessed at by looking at the eyes. Ideally, the horse will have large eyes set well to each side of his head. This enables him to have good binocular vision and excellent monocular vision.

Eyes that are soft and gentle in appearance indicate that the horse has a quiet personality and will tend to look calmly about his environment instead of rolling his eyes so that the white sclera is visible. When a horse's eyes roll in that manner, it indicates that he is fright-

## The Vice Squad

HORSES ARE PROGRAMMED to move around and graze for most of the day and night, so being confined for long periods of time is unnatural and may understandably create discomfort, boredom, or restlessness. Some horses develop behaviors that seem intended to relieve distress but with extensive repetition can actually be harmful. These behaviors, or stereotypes, are called "stable vices" and have been compared with compulsive behavior in humans. Some research indicates that performing these repetitive behaviors releases chemicals in the brain that relieve stress or cause pleasure.

Many horse owners believe that foals learn vices from their dams and that older horses will learn from stablemates, but there is little evidence that these behaviors are acquired by imitation. They do seem to start when a young horse is kept in a stall for long hours without much opportunity to graze or exercise.

Here are some of the more common vices.

Cribbing. The horse bites onto the edge of a stall door or other horizontal piece of wood and holds on while tightening his neck and sucking in air, making a burping or grunting sound. Cribbing can lead to colic and tooth damage. It is nearly impossible to cure a cribber; the behavior can be stopped with the use of a cribbing strap that buckles around the throat,

ened or, in some cases, inherently nervous and flighty. This doesn't mean that seeing white in the horse's eye automatically indicates instability. Conformation is part of the equation. Some horses, such as Appaloosas, naturally have eyes with a good deal of sclera visible.

Equine eyes that are small and set close together sometimes indicate an aggressive, stubborn, or difficult character, although this isn't true of every horse. The fact that eyes so constructed provide poor peripheral vision could influence the horse's reaction to his environment, causing him to be apprehensive and suspicious.

> **FAST FACT** A horse with very small eyes is said to be "pig-eyed," and a horse with blue eyes is called "wall-eyed."

making it uncomfortable to contract the neck muscles. Some research indicates that cribbers are more likely to suffer from an imbalance in stomach acid; a change of diet and antiacid medication may help.

**Wood chewing.** The horse chews at wooden fencing, walls, and feeders and can cause extensive damage. Though sometimes indicative of boredom, this behavior can also result from a lack of roughage in the diet and can be helped by offering more hay.

**Weaving and stall walking.** The horse stands in one spot and weaves from side to side on his front legs or paces restlessly from one side of his stall or pen to the other. A horse who weaves or walks excessively may require extra food so that he doesn't lose weight from expending too much energy. More exercise and outside turnout can help.

**Pawing.** The horse paws steadily, sometimes out of boredom, until it creates a depression or hole in the ground or stall floor. This can lead to wearing down of the front hooves or loss of a shoe, as well as possible damage to the legs. Providing more exercise and not overfeeding may cure a horse of pawing.

**Kicking.** The horse kicks the stall wall when confined, causing damage to the stall and his rear hooves. More exercise and other stimulation can help; there are also mechanical devices, such as a light chain suspended from the horse's middle, that discourage kicking by giving a mild correction when the foot is lifted.

## Q Are horses afraid of water?

**A** When asked to cross water, horses often are apprehensive because they are unable to determine how deep it is or how solid the footing is until they set foot on it. They must be taught to trust the rider and follow her cues. Generally speaking, the muddier the water, the more apprehensive the horse. If the water is shallow and flowing over a visible bottom, the horse often realizes that it poses no danger. Deep water or a swift current that makes it difficult for the horse to focus on the bottom may also make him nervous. (See *Can horses swim?*, page 195.)

## Boys Will Be Boys

MOST MALE HORSES these days are castrated because it makes them more tractable and easier to handle, as well as eliminating the possibility of breeding. Gelding can take place when the colt is a few weeks old. The older the colt, the more stallion-like his physique and behavior will be; even after castration, some of those attributes will remain.

In fact, old-time horse people had a term for geldings who continue to exhibit stallion-like behavior: "**proud cut.**" They believed that a testicular component that produced testosterone had not been removed. Although possible in days gone by, this situation would be extremely rare today with modern castration techniques. A more likely explanation is that the problem gelding is producing excess testosterone from his adrenal glands.

Normally, the testicles of a male fetus descend into the scrotum about 30 days before birth. In some cases, the testicle is unable to descend through the inguinal canal and remains lodged in the abdomen. The scientific term is **cryptorchid**; the colloquial is **ridgling**. The ridgling horse is sterile because the abdominal body temperature is too high for sperm to survive. Unless surgically removed, however, the lodged testicle is capable of producing testosterone, which may stimulate stallion-like behavior.

*A well-trained horse will "shy in place," meaning that he jumps or startles, but will not attempt to flee the scene.*

## Q What does it mean when a horse "shies"?

A To shy or spook means that the horse moves suddenly to avoid a scary object or sound. He might leap sideways, bolt forward, or back up rapidly to put space between himself and the perceived threat. Some horses have more of a tendency to shy than others.

## Q What does "headshy" mean?

A The headshy horse is afraid of having his head touched and will jerk back or raise his head to avoid contact. This obviously makes it difficult to handle the animal for haltering or bridling, grooming, or giving medication. This condition generally results from mistreatment or rough handling. Curing headshyness is possible, but it takes repetition and patience to convince the horse that human contact doesn't always cause pain.

# CHAPTER FOUR

# BREEDS

# How to Tell a Saddlebred from a Standardbred

S oon after humans domesticated horses, they learned to breed selectively for desired traits. Horses had already developed distinct characteristics as they adapted to different environments. In cold climates, for example, they had thicker skins, warm winter coats, and smaller statures. Desert denizens needed thinner skin to keep cool, longer legs to raise their bodies above the hot sand, and the ability to survive on little water. Humans bred animals with specific physical and personality attributes to create distinct breeds over generations. Today there are hundreds of different breeds, some spread around the world and others numbering only in the dozens and living in isolated herds.

## Q What's the difference between a breed and a species?

**A** A **breed** is a particular type of horse with a set of recognizable physical characteristics that have been determined over generations of deliberate selection by humans. The term "breed" typically applies to purebred horses and ponies whose bloodlines are recorded in a breed registry.

Different breeds show many variations in size, color, strength, speed, and personality, but all breeds of horses can mate with each other to produce fertile offspring because all belong to the same genus and species, *E. caballus*, which means they share the same genetic material (DNA). (See *Is there more than one species of equine?*, page 2.)

## Q What is a breed registry?

**A** Also called a **studbook**, a breed registry is an official list of individual animals who conform to the standards of a particular breed. The registry certifies the pedigree of each animal, including a description of how it meets the standards for the breed for size, proportion, color, and specific features. In most cases, a foal can be registered only if both the sire and the dam are of the same breed, although some breed registries accept horses with one only registered parent.

Some registries accept individuals based solely or primarily on physical appearance or ability. Color breeds, like Palomino, Buckskin, and Pinto, for example, may be registered as a specific breed (Quarter Horse) and also with a registry based on color. Some gaited horse registries accept individuals because they have the ability to move with a particular gait.

> ‖ FAST FACT The practice of registering purebred horses began
> ‖ in 1791 with the publication of the General Stud Book in the
> ‖ United Kingdom.

# Q How many breeds of horses are there in the world?

A Worldwide, several hundred distinct breeds exist, many with their own registries, but a firm number is difficult to establish because some local breeds are not well documented or known outside their native lands, and a number of documented breeds have become extinct or have very few remaining individuals.

# Q Are there horse breeds that no longer exist?

A Around the world, many breeds of feral horses, often numbering only a few hundred individuals, have disappeared as their habitat has been developed for human use. Many specific domestic types or breeds have also been lost over the years as human need for and use of the horse changed. The all-purpose **Chapman Horse**, developed in England, was so heavily crossbred with imported horses to create a breed more suitable for pulling carriages that the original breed became extinct. The **Galloway Pony**, once native to Scotland and northern England, suffered a similar fate when local farmers bred these small, hardy ponies to develop heavier, stronger horses who could serve as draft horses.

Breeds also risk extinction when people lose interest in producing them. **Karacabey Horses** originated in Turkey hundreds of years ago as a cross between the Turkish Arab racehorse and the local Anadolu. They became international favorites as polo horses and jumpers, but by 1980, the Karacabey stud had ceased all breeding because of competition from high-quality horses from France and Germany.

**Przewalski's Horse**, considered the last of the truly wild horses on earth, almost became extinct from loss of habitat, being hunted for food, and interbreeding with domestic horses. Last seen in the wild in 1969, they have survived in captivity thanks to a successful breeding program in Mongolia, and several hundred have been reintroduced to managed wildlife areas in other parts of the world. (See *The Last Truly Wild Horse*, page 192, and *The Rise and Fall of the Narragansett Pacer*, page 83.)

## A NEAR-DEATH EXPERIENCE

The small **Caspian Horse** is an ancient breed that originated in Iran. It had been thought to be extinct for over a thousand years, but in 1965, Louise Firouz, an American living in Iran, came across three beautiful specimens in an area near the Caspian Sea. She began a search for more individuals, locating 20 more over a 5-year period.

The small herd that Firouz was developing and studying was attacked by wolves during the summer of 1976, and three mares and a foal were killed. To preserve the breed, seven mares and a stallion were flown to England and placed with a stud farm in Shropshire. Political upheaval in Iran threatened the breed even more, and some were exported to Texas, where several hundred now live. The Caspian, although still quite rare, is no longer in danger of extinction.

Standing between 10 and 12 hands tall, Caspians have the typically agreeable temperament found in small horses, plus a natural jumping ability and a smooth pace. Their grace and intelligence make them desirable and successful in the show ring and as harness horses.

**Q** Which are the most popular breeds in the United States?

**A** In the United States, the American Quarter Horse is the most popular by a wide margin, with nearly 3 million horses registered. The Paint Horse is the second most popular pleasure horse, with almost 1 million registered. Thoroughbreds, bred primarily for racing, have about the same population as Paints, keeping in mind that the population of each breed changes as new horses are registered each year. From there, the numbers drop off quite drastically, with Arabians, Appaloosas, and Morgans following in roughly that order.

FAST FACT **Worldwide, the three most popular breeds are the Arabian, the American Quarter Horse, and the Paint.**

# The Story of Steel Dust

**STEEL DUST** was one of the horses who set the standard for what would become the official Quarter Horse breed. Details of Steel Dust's birth are a bit hazy. Some reports say he was foaled in Kentucky, while others claim it was Illinois, but it is generally agreed that he was foaled in 1843. Purchased at a young age by two Texans, Steel Dust matured into a handsome, powerfully built bay stallion, standing 15 hands high and weighing about 1,200 pounds (544 kg). His fame spread as he demonstrated that he could run faster than any challengers.

His final race was to be against Shiloh, a stellar racehorse from Tennessee. The race was held in Dallas, where the racetrack was state-of-the-art for that period. Instead of sending the racers off from a line in the ground, the Dallas track featured a starting gate with chutes, and the straightaway was free of the rocks, stumps, and other obstructions that were common to most tracks.

As the two stallions awaited the signal to start, Steel Dust became excited and reared up against the chute. A board broke, puncturing his shoulder. The race was called off, but Steel Dust lived a full life, putting his stamp on a number of foals before dying in the late 1860s.

Horses with Steel Dust blood became highly desired as ranch and rodeo horses and, as years went by, horses who merely resembled him in appearance were called Steel Dusts, often with the goal of a higher purchase price. It wasn't until the American Quarter Horse Association (AQHA) was formed in 1940 that the Steel Dust name began to fade from existence, being replaced by Quarter Horse.

*The versatile American Quarter Horse is by far the most popular breed in the United States, and one of the top three in the world.*

# Q Is a Quarter Horse one-fourth of another breed?

**A** The American Quarter Horse is consistent and versatile, making it the most popular and populous breed of horses in the world, with more than 5 million registered worldwide. This first truly American breed originated in eastern colonies in the 1700s from a combination of European horses, Chickasaw Indian horses, and the horses of the Spanish conquistadores.

These powerfully built horses excelled at sprinting, and were often raced on a straight, quarter-mile (0.4 km) track, which earned them the name Quarter Miler or Quarter Horse. The breed also demonstrated a natural instinct for working around cattle ("cow sense"), and was often the choice of cowboys and pioneers as they expanded the country westward in the 1800s.

Quarter Horses continue to be agile, sturdy, intelligent, and willing to work. Their friendly, even temperament makes them popular with beginners and they are wonderful pleasure horses for trail riding. Many still work on ranches and are used in rodeos, for racing, and as show horses.

The American Quarter Horse Association (AQHA) recognizes 13 colors for the breed, including bay, black, palomino, buckskin, and gray, but sorrel (chestnut) is the most common color. There are two types: the stock type, which is compact and muscular, and the racing type, which is slightly taller with smoother muscles.

> **FAST FACT** **Quarter Horses have been clocked doing 55 mph (88.5 km/h) and can outrun a Thoroughbred over a short distance.**

## Q What is an Appendix Quarter Horse?

A After the AQHA was established (see previous question), breeders debated how much Thoroughbred blood should be allowed in the registry. Because some of the foundation bloodlines came from Thoroughbreds, one contingent took the position that unlimited Thoroughbred blood should be permitted in registered Quarter Horses. In the early days of the registry, inspectors traveled around the country examining horses whose owners sought to include them, but in the early 1960s, the AQHA "closed the book" and ruled that only foals of registered Quarter Horse parents could be registered in the future.

The registry accommodated the pro-Thoroughbred contingent by establishing an Appendix registration for the offspring of a registered Thoroughbred mated with a registered Quarter Horse, or the offspring of an Appendix horse mated with a registered Quarter Horse. Appendix horses are allowed to compete in Quarter Horse shows and races.

Appendix horses can earn their way into the permanent AQHA registry by accumulating a certain number of points in the show ring or on the race track. The registration number of Appendix horses carries an "X."

*My treasures do not clink together or glitter; they gleam in the sun and neigh in the night.*

— ARABIAN PROVERB

# The Aristocratic Arabian

**THE ARABIAN HORSE** is the oldest known breed of riding horse, originating over 4,000 years ago in the deserts of the Middle East. Bedouin tribesmen bred these elegant horses for strength and endurance on long treks through the desert, and for courage and speed in battle. Because of their beauty, character, and stamina, breeders worldwide have used Arabian blood over the centuries to improve the quality of local horses. Arabians were instrumental in establishing the Thoroughbred, for example (see *Who are the Founding Fathers?*, page 93).

A small horse, averaging 14 to 15.3 hands, the Arabian is readily recognized by its characteristic dished face and high-set tail carriage. It has large eyes, a wide forehead, and small ears that should curve at the tips. The color may be bay, chestnut, gray, black, or roan, and they always have black skin. White markings are permitted, but never pinto or spotted coloring. Arabians are exceptional endurance and pleasure horses, but are also seen doing dressage, racing, and even working cattle.

The first Arabian stallion in North America was imported to Virginia in 1725 and sired 300 foals with local mares. In 1888, two imported Arabian mares were bred with an Arabian stallion that had been a gift to Ulysses S. Grant from the Sultan of Turkey, starting the first line of purebred Arabians in the United States.

## Q Do any horse breeds suffer from genetic problems the way many dog breeds do?

A Whenever humans breed individual animals for desired traits and keep breeding within the same bloodlines to develop a particular type of horse, dog, or any other animal, there is a risk of genetic mutation. Undesirable traits are passed along just as "good" traits (build, size, speed, coat color) are, and sometimes there is a link between the two, as with the risk of impaired hearing found in many American Paint horses with blue eyes and certain coat patterns.

Genetic testing is available for many of these conditions, and others are being developed so that breeders can avoid pairing horses who are likely to produce damaged foals. Here is a partial list of some other breeds with potential genetic defects:

◆ A particular line of Quarter Horses, bred primarily for halter classes, carries a gene for hyperkalcemic periodic paralysis (HYPP), a condition that causes weakness and muscle tremors.

◆ A genetic mutation found in Paints and Quarter Horses can lead to overo lethal white syndrome, in which the all-white offspring suffers from severe intestinal abnormalities and dies soon after birth.

◆ The silver coat that is considered a desirable trait in Rocky Mountain horses and some other breeds is associated with eye defects.

◆ Equine recurrent uveitis (moon blindness), an inflammation of the eye, affects just 1 to 2 percent of the general population, but nearly a quarter of Appaloosas are vulnerable.

◆ Some Belgians and American Saddlebreds suffer from genetic mutations that can result in a lethal skin condition.

FAST FACT **Although white horses are more vulnerable to skin cancer and eye problems, their light-colored coats make them less attractive to blood-sucking, disease-spreading horseflies and deerflies.**

## THE RISE AND FALL OF
## THE NARRAGANSETT PACER

For nearly 150 years, the now-extinct Narragansett Pacer was the most popular saddle horse in the American colonies. A pacer has a smooth, natural gait that makes for a comfortable ride, and at the time of the American Revolution, this was the most desirable horse in North America. Paul Revere rode one on his famous ride, and the breed was said to be a favorite mount of George Washington. (See *What's the difference between trotting and pacing?*, page 149.)

First developed in the Narragansett Bay region of Rhode Island, they were small horses, standing about 14 hands high, but hardy and sure-footed with excellent speed and stamina. They were, however, neither stylish nor handsome, which probably contributed to their going out of fashion as the advent of wheeled coaches and carriages vastly reduced the demand for riding horses.

Pacers were crossbred with Thoroughbreds in America and with Spanish stock in the West Indies. By 1800, the Narragansett Pacer had been bred out of existence, but many of its valuable qualities were passed along to other breeds, including the modern Paso, the Standardbred, the Tennessee Walking Horse, the American Saddlebred, and the Canadian Horse.

## Q What is a "light" horse?

A In contrast to large, heavy draft horses, light horses are the riding or driving breeds. They vary greatly in color and conformation, but their common characteristic is that they are trainable and comfortable to ride. There are far more light horse breeds than draft horses or ponies.

FAST FACT In the trot, the diagonal legs move together (left hind/ right front; right hind/ left front), whereas in the pace, the lateral pairs move together (left hind/front; right hind/front).

## Q What is the largest breed of horse? The smallest?

A The largest horses obviously come from the draft breeds, and over the years, many horses have claimed the individual record based on height or weight. **Shires** are the tallest breed, with some individuals reaching over 20 hands, while the massive **Brabant**, originally from Belgium and weighing as much as 3,000 pounds (1,361 kg), trots off with first place for heaviest breed.

The smallest horses are miniature breeds, with the **Falabella** being the tiniest. Miniature horses are measured not in hands, but in inches from the endpoint of the mane, and most mature Falabellas measure from 30 to 34 inches (76–86 cm) high, although they can be as small as 25 inches (64 cm).

*While horse breeds do not demonstrate the extreme differences in body types that dog breeds do, the difference in size between a Miniature Horse and a Shire is considerable.*

**Q** What do you get if you cross a hot-blooded horse with a cold-blooded one?

**A** Like mixing hot and cold tap water, you'd produce a warmblood. All horses have the same average body temperature (see *Vital Signs*, page 28). These descriptive categories refer instead to types of horses based on conformation, temperament, and usage.

So-called **hot-blooded horses** are small- to medium-sized and lightly built. They are fast and agile, and considered more excitable and reactive than other types, although also noted for their intelligence and courage. The versatile Arabian and the valiant Thoroughbred are typical hot-blooded breeds.

**Cold-blooded horses** are generally large, heavy, and powerful, with calm temperaments and willing natures; these are the draft breeds, typified by the Clydesdale and the Belgian. Some of the bigger, more muscular pony breeds also fall into this category. Many of these breeds were originally developed as warhorses to safely carry a heavily armed rider under battlefield conditions.

As you might expect, **warm-blooded horses** combine characteristics of both types. These breeds, which include the Hanoverian and the Trakehner, were specifically developed to excel at performance sports such as dressage and show jumping. Often referred to as "sport horses," warmbloods also make excellent mounts for hunting and cross-country riding, and many are exceptional harness horses. These outstanding athletes have strong personalities, with plenty of stamina, energy, and willingness to match.

# All-American Drafts

**A DRAFT HORSE OR A DRAY** (from the Anglo-Saxon *dragan,* meaning to draw or haul) is a large, muscular horse with a docile temperament that has been bred to perform heavy tasks like plowing, logging, and hauling. Found in many different parts of the world, most draft breeds have ancient histories; without them, human civilization would have taken a very different course.

Almost all modern breeds of draft horses originated in Europe. Historians have concluded that the first heavy horse was a type known as the Black Horse of Flanders, developed in the lowlands of what is now France and Belgium. The Flanders horse was refined into the modern-day Percheron and was a wellspring for other draft breeds.

*Though draft horses are notable for their heavy muscling, large size, and great strength, they are also known for their gentle and willing natures.*

Some of the better-known modern draft horse breeds include the Percheron (a French breed that can still be seen in circus vaulting acts), the Clydesdale (of Budweiser fame, although originally from Scotland), and the Belgian (the most common draft horse in North America). Following are profiles of two breeds that were "born in the USA."

The American Cream Draft Horse, the only draft horse breed that claims to be native to the United States, traces its origin to a foundation mare who lived in central Iowa in the early 1900s. Old Granny, as she was known, was a farm animal with the cream-colored coat, pink skin, and amber eyes that are characteristic of the breed. The American Cream Horse Association of America was granted a charter by the State of Iowa in 1944, but as farmers replaced their draft animals with tractors, the breed almost became extinct. In 1982, several breeders initiated a successful effort to register the remaining horses and increase their numbers, though they are still quite rare, with just a few hundred in existence.

The North American Spotted Draft is an even more recent breed, with the studbook being established in 1995. Large horses with spotted coloring were used in Europe as warhorses in medieval times and they have a long history in the United States as well. Spotted drafts should have conformation that reflects one of the draft breeds (often Belgian or Percheron). They are large, strong, and muscular, ranging from 16 to more than 17 hands high.

They have pinto coloring in one of the typical patterns, and any base color is acceptable, although black, bay, and brown are the most common. Somewhat lighter in weight than other draft breeds, these horses are popular in the show ring and for pulling commercial carriages, as well as for logging, farm work, pleasure driving, and riding.

# Q What are color breeds?

A Some breed registries accept horses from virtually any breed as long as they match certain color requirements. Not included in this category are purebred horses whose distinctive color is part of the breed standard: the Friesian (black), the Cleveland Bay (bay), and the Haflinger (chestnut).

Horses that are registered as a color breed are often also registered with a specific breed association. A buckskin Quarter Horse, for example, might be registered with both the American Quarter Horse Association and the International Buckskin Horse Association. The offspring of two registered horses that doesn't inherit the correct color might not be accepted by its parent's registry. Official color breeds include buckskin, palomino, and pinto.

The ideal shade of **buckskin** is the color of tanned deer hide, although shades ranging from cream to dark gold are accepted. The mane, tail, and lower legs must be black. The International Buckskin Horse Association registers horses of any breed that are buckskin, dun (somewhat duller than buckskin), red dun (dun color on a chestnut body), and grulla or blue dun (dun on a darker body). The dun factor is a gene that contributes to the dark points found on the buckskin; duns have a dorsal stripe and some have striping on their legs.

**Palomino** describes a golden horse with a white mane and tail. These horses have black skin, with only a certain amount of white markings allowed. Known and prized for centuries, palominos often served as the mounts for royalty because of their beauty and elegance. A related color is cremello, an extremely pale yellow that results from a dilution gene that lightens whatever color is present.

**Pintos** are perhaps the most easily recognized color breed, with their distinctive splotched coats of white and

FAST FACT **Though common in dogs and cattle, brindled coloring (mottled stripes) is very rare in horses. The American Quarter Horse Association registers only a dozen or so horses that can be described as brindles, out of several million.**

black or white and brown. Pinto coloring has been present in horses from ancient times but humans have valued it differently in different eras. (See *What's the difference between a pinto and a Paint?*, page 100, and *Congratulations — It's a Bay!*, pages 6–7.)

## Q What are some gaited breeds?

A In addition to the usual walk, trot, and canter, gaited horses naturally perform additional gaits that usually provide an exceptionally comfortable ride (see *What is a "gaited horse"?*, page 18.) There are many different breeds of gaited horses, which typically offer both a four-beat ambling gait and a smooth, intermediate speed. The exact style, footfall pattern, and name of these gaits vary among breeds. Some breeds do the same gait at different speeds; the Icelandic Horse, for example, *tolts* about as fast as a regular trot, but moves as fast as a gallop at the *skeith*.

This natural tendency to be gaited, found in breeds all over the world, has been noted for many centuries. When humans primarily rode instead of driving horses, gaited animals were highly prized by people such as plantation owners and cowboys, who spent many hours in the saddle. Today, gaited horses such as the Missouri Fox Trotter and the Tennessee Walking Horse are popular trail and pleasure mounts. (See the following question and *What is a Missouri Fox Trotter?*, page 99; *The Florida Cracker*, page 98; *Are a Paso Fino and a Peruvian Paso the same breed?*, page 99; *Can Tennessee Walkers trot and canter?*, page 102; *What is a "Big Lick" Horse?*, page 186.)

## Q Which breed is known as the "Peacock of the Show Ring"?

A With its flowing tail, arched neck, and flaring nostrils, the American Saddlebred provides flash and excitement as it performs its high-stepping gaits, reminding observers of a gaudy peacock strutting his stuff. The foundation bloodlines of this breed came from natural pacers, called Galloway and Hobby horses, brought to North America by British colonists. The Narragansett Pacer (see *The Rise and Fall of the Narragansett Pacer*, page 83) was also important in establishing the breed, which, known as the American Horse, was well established by the time of the American Revolution.

*For the show ring, the Saddlebred's characteristic long tail is often enhanced with extensions.*

Saddlebreds appeared in the show ring for the first time in 1903 in Missouri and have continued to wow crowds with their flashy presence as they perform the walk, trot, canter, slow gait, and rack. The slow gait is a balanced way of going that suspends the horse's entire weight onto one foot at a time. The rack is the same gait performed at speed. These show gaits are sometimes enhanced by the use of built-up shoes and controversial training methods.

A finely built horse with a wide chest and short back, the Saddlebred comes in all colors. They compete in activities that range from dressage and show jumping to cutting and reining.

## Q What is standard about a Standardbred?

A The first trotting races were conducted under saddle, with the racecourse often being the length of an open field. By the middle of the eighteenth century, trotters competed on established courses with the horses pulling lightweight carts called **sulkies**. By then, breeders had developed a strong trotting horse from a mixture of breeds, including the Narragansett Pacer, English Thoroughbred, Norfolk Trotter, Hackney, and Morgan.

A studbook for trotters and pacers established in 1871 required that, to be registered, a horse must be able to meet a standard time over 1 mile (1.6 km), which was 2.5 minutes for the trot and 2.25 minutes for the pace, times now considered training speeds. (See *What's the difference between trotting and pacing?*, page 149.) The U.S. Trotting Association was created in 1939 to formulate racing rules and regulations and establish a registry for the Standardbred, and today, all Standardbreds must have registered parents to be registered with the association.

Standardbreds are known for their calm temperaments. Although bred to be competitive, they make excellent saddle and trail horses even after a racing career. They resemble Thoroughbreds but are usually somewhat smaller, with longer bodies, heavier muscles, and long, straight profiles. They can be any solid color, but are typically bay, brown, or black.

*Harness races for trotters and pacers are popular in various parts of the United States. A horse that breaks its stride may remain in the race but must be steered clear of the field and returned to the required gait.*

## THE STORY OF HAMBLETONIAN 10

The cornerstone of the Standardbred breed was a gray English Thoroughbred named Messenger who arrived in the United States in 1788. His lineage traces to the Darley Arabian, one of the foundation sires of the modern Thoroughbred (see *Who are the Founding Fathers?*, facing page). One of his descendents, Hambletonian 10, was foaled in 1849 in New York. As a youngster, Hambletonian was not all that impressive, and he and his dam were sold for $125 to a young farmhand named William Rysdyk.

Although he never raced, Hambletonian stood at stud from age 2 until his death at age 27, and sired more than 1,300 offspring — in 1864 alone he bred 217 mares. A great many of his offspring were excellent trotters and pacers, and Hambletonian's fame spread, earning Rysdyk close to half a million dollars in breeding fees during the horse's lifetime. Today, the pedigrees of some 90 percent of all Standardbreds trace back to Hambletonian 10, and at one time, the whole breed was called Hambletonians.

# Q Who are the Founding Fathers?

A The three horses described below are the foundation sires of the modern Thoroughbred. The pedigree of every modern Thoroughbred goes back to one of these stallions and to one of 74 foundation mares.

The Godolphin Arabian is also known as the Godolphin Barb, suggesting his origin might have been on the Barbary Coast of Tunisia or Morocco. He was a pure bay, one of nine horses sent as a gift to King Louis XV from the Bey of Tunis, and was imported from France in 1730 by Edward Coke. He is named for the second Earl of Godolphin, who bought him from Coke's heir and sent him to stud.

The Byerley Turk was said to have been taken from a Turkish officer by Captain Robert Byerley at the siege of Buda in 1688 and sent to England. He was an unmarked dark brown horse with the conformation of an Arabian. In 1690 he won the top prize in a race at Down Royal in Northern Ireland. Later the same year, he served as the Captain's mount during the battle of the Boyne in Ireland against the forces of King James II.

The Darley Arabian was a bay colt owned by Bedouin Sheikh Mirza II, who lived in the Syrian desert. Thomas Darley, the British consul, had agreed to buy the horse in 1704, but the sheikh apparently changed his mind about parting with his finest colt and Darley is said to have arranged to have the colt smuggled out of the country and delivered to England, where he stood at stud until 1719.

# Q What's the difference between a Thoroughbred and a purebred?

A The term "purebred" describes an animal from a particular breed, as in a purebred Arabian, a purebred Dalmatian, or a purebred Siamese cat. A Thoroughbred is a specific horse breed that was developed for racing in England in the early eighteenth century. (See *How far back in history does horse racing go?*, page 135.)

Approximately 30,000 Thoroughbreds are registered annually in the United States, although not all are bound for the racetrack. With their speed, strength, coordination, and drive (known as "heart"),

Thoroughbreds excel at show jumping, fox hunting, dressage, polo, and many other riding disciplines.

Ranging from 15 to 17 hands, most Thoroughbreds are long and lean, with small heads set on long necks. They have thin skin and fine hair and may be bay, chestnut, black, or gray, often with white markings on the face and legs. Pinto coloring is allowed but not very common.

## Q Are all Appaloosas spotted?

A One of the most popular breeds in the United States, an Appaloosa is characterized by its unique spotted coat and mottled skin. The Appaloosa breed registry recognizes 13 base coat colors, ranging from black to buckskin, which can be overlaid by any of several different patterns, including **blanket** (a large patch of solid white or white with spots, usually over the hips) and **leopard** (many small spots scattered over the whole body). Some Appys, as they are often called, have very few spots, while others are splashed all over with them.

Spanish conquistadors brought spotted horses to the New World beginning in the early 1500s. They were captured in various parts of the country by indigenous tribes, but the Nez Perce of the Pacific Northwest are credited with developing the breed. They were concentrated in the area of the Palouse River, giving them the name Palouse horses, which eventually became Appaloosa.

The Indians used them as workhorses, racehorses, and war mounts. During the late 1800s, the United States cavalry fought the Nez Perce for many months, with the result that many Appaloosas were abandoned, killed, and gelded, causing the breed to almost disappear. Renewed interest in these strong and versatile horses in the early 1900s has resulted in almost 750,000 Appaloosas registered worldwide.

|| FAST FACT **Spotted horses appear in cave paintings in France that date back more than 20,000 years.**

**LEOPARD**

*Appaloosas appear in an astonishing variety of coat patterns, each one unique. In addition to their spots, Appaloosas typically have striped hooves, mottled skin around their muzzles, and some white showing around the iris of their eyes. Their manes and tails tend to be sparser than other breeds.*

**BLANKET**

## Q What can Lipizzans do that other breeds can't?

A The Lipizzan or Lipizzaner was developed from ancient Spanish bloodlines crossed with Barbs and Arabs during the 700-year occupation of Spain by the Moors. Brought to Austria in the late sixteenth century, the breed's name comes from a stud farm founded in Lipizza, in what is now Slovenia, by Archduke Charles. Today's horses descend from 6 carefully selected stallions and just 16 mares.

Intelligent, strong, and sturdily built, Lipizzans undergo years of careful training to learn their "airs above the ground," a level of dressage movement unmatched by any other breed. They are also prized for pleasure riding and other equestrian disciplines. The first Lipizzans were imported into the United States in the 1930s and their numbers have slowly increased, although there are only about 3,000 purebred Lipizzans in the world. (See *The Cavalry to the Rescue*, below. See *Airs Above the Ground*, page 184.)

FAST FACT Like all gray horses, Lipizzan foals are born dark and attain their characteristic white coat between the ages of 6 and 10. Very infrequently, a bay Lippazan is born.

### THE CAVALRY TO THE RESCUE

As fighting neared Vienna in 1945, officials of the famed Spanish Riding School moved their precious Lipizzan stallions to the Austrian countryside. General George Patton saw the horses perform and was prevailed upon to put them under the protection of the U.S. Army. When the United States Second Cavalry, a tank division, occupied Hostau, Czechoslovakia, in 1945, it discovered several hundred Lipizzan mares and foals that had been stolen by the Nazis. It took a number of years, but eventually the breeding stock was returned to its home in Piber and the stallions to Vienna, where they perform to this day.

*Justin Morgan is the only horse known as the sole progenitor of a breed. All Morgans trace their lineage to him.*

## Q Who was Justin Morgan?

**A** The original Justin Morgan was a man, but his name became synonymous with the only breed of horse called after a person. Justin Morgan was a schoolteacher, composer, and for a while the town clerk in Randolph, Vermont. He was also a farmer and horse breeder, standing stallions at stud in various locales. In payment of a debt in 1792, he received a small bay stallion that he named Figure. He only owned the colt for three years, but during that time, the sturdy little horse gained the reputation of being able to out-trot, outpull, outrun, and outwalk any horse who was put against him.

And it soon became apparent that Figure was phenomenally prepotent, meaning that he put his stamp on his offspring, no matter what type of mare was involved in the mating. It wasn't long before owners were coming from far and wide to breed their mares to this unusual horse. During his lifetime, his stud services were offered throughout the Connecticut River Valley and parts of Vermont.

Figure stood only about 14 hands and weighed around 900 pounds (408 kg), but he was both beautiful and powerful. His ancestry is debatable, but many believe his sire was a fine English stallion named True Briton. One story has it that True Briton was stolen by colonists during the Revolutionary War while his owner, a Tory commander, was drinking in a tavern. The thieves then sold True Briton to a farmer in Connecticut, eventually leading to the birth of Figure in West Springfield, Massachusetts, in 1789.

After Justin Morgan traded him for some land, Figure became known as the Justin Morgan horse and later simply took on the name of his former owner. Throughout his lifetime, the horse had many owners, most of whom used him to pull farm implements or haul freight as well as serve as a stud. He died at the age of 32 after suffering injuries from being kicked by another horse.

## THE FLORIDA CRACKER — NOT A SNACK

The Florida Cracker, though one of the oldest breeds in the United States, is now extremely rare, with fewer than 1,000 individuals registered. Descended from early Spanish horses, these tough little horses were used in the Florida cattle industry for centuries. The cattle drivers used long, snapping whips to move their herds of tough, wily cows through the brush, hence the name "crackers." The horses they rode had strong cow sense, matched with great agility, speed, and hardiness. The Florida Cracker is a small horse, sometimes referred to as a pony, that is naturally gaited, giving a comfortable ride while covering a lot of ground.

A government program in the 1930s that encouraged the movement of cattle from the drought-stricken West into the southern states nearly caused the demise of the breed. The western cattle were larger than the Florida cows, requiring larger horses to manage them. As Quarter Horses replaced Crackers, the breed almost disappeared. Interested owners came together in the 1980s to form a registry and establish bloodlines.

The Florida Cracker was declared the official horse of Florida in 2008.

## Q What is a Missouri Fox Trotter?

A This gentle gaited horse is known to be particularly sure-footed and comfortable to ride. A Missouri Fox Trotter has three natural gaits: an easygoing flat-footed walk, the smooth and comfortable diagonal four-beat fox trot from which its name is derived, and a relaxed, free-flowing canter.

The breed was developed in the Missouri Ozarks from horses that were brought there by early settlers from neighboring states. They are valued for trail riding, for Western competition, and as show horses. Elegant yet sturdy, they can be pinto or solid; shades of palomino and champagne are common.

## Q Are a Paso Fino and a Peruvian Paso the same breed?

A *Paso* means "step" in Spanish and although these distinct breeds are both naturally gaited, they have quite different histories. The Paso Fino are intelligent and hardy animals that originated from horses imported to the Caribbean from Spain. They range widely in size and color, which can include pinto and palomino markings.

*Paso Finos* are valued as competitive trail horses for their smooth and comfortable ride and their *brio* or proud, spirited bearing. They perform a four-beat, lateral gait in which the sequence of the footfalls is right rear, right front, left rear, left front. It is performed at three speeds in three styles: the slow Classic Fino, the looser Paso Corto, and the speedy Paso Largo.

The *Peruvian Paso* hails from Peru, where it was developed from several Old World breeds to provide horses able to carry overseers long distances across huge sugar and cotton plantations in the north and through the southern deserts. Like the Paso Fino, the Peruvian Paso inherits its ability to gait and cannot be trained into it. The breed is remarkable for its brilliant action, called *termino*, characterized by high knee lift and a rolling motion of the front legs that can be compared to that of a swimmer's arms.

# Q What's the difference between a pinto and a Paint?

A While colorful horses with splotches of white are often associated with the American Indian, horses with spotted coats have been known around the world for centuries. They arrived in North America with the Spanish explorers. The terms "paint" and "pinto" are often used interchangeably, but they mean two different things.

Pinto refers only to the color pattern, which can appear in many different breeds, including the Quarter Horse; Mustangs and other Spanish-type breeds; some gaited horses; a few pony breeds; and many warmblood breeds. The Pinto Horse Association of America requires a certain amount of white hair over unpigmented (pink) skin combined with any other color of the equine spectrum. Specific coat patterns such as **overo** (mostly color with white patches) and **tobiano**

*Many breed standards specifically prohibit splashy pinto coloring, but a variety of breed registries accept it. Breeds that allow it include the shaggy little Icelandic Horse, the elegant Tennessee Walker, and the Gypsy Vanner, a magnificent horse whose striking coat is set off by a flowing mane and tail and abundant leg feathering.*

(mostly white with colored patches) are described. Other characteristics include white on the legs extending above the knee, white or parti-colored hooves, and blue eyes.

The American Paint Horse, in contrast, is an established breed of stock-type (working) horse. To be eligible for the breed registry, at least one parent must be a registered Paint, while the other can be a registered Paint, Quarter Horse, or Thoroughbred. Pinto coloring is desirable, but not necessary for registration.

## The Myth of the Medicine Hat

**A TYPE OF PINTO,** medicine hat horses are usually predominantly white, with dark ears and what looks like a hat (or war bonnet) covering the top of their head and their ears. Some have a large dark mark on the chest, called a shield, and some have other pinto markings. Many have one or two blue eyes.

True medicine hat coloring is quite rare, and historically, some Native American tribes prized these horses, which were believed to possess the power to make their riders invincible in battle. They are still considered by many to bring luck to their owners.

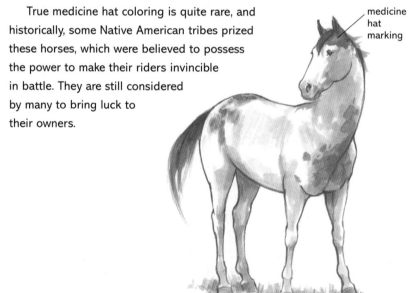

medicine hat marking

## SWEATING BLOOD

The Akhal-Teke is a breed of horse that is thought to have descended from an ancient Scythian light-bodied horse of the arid deserts of central Asia. They were highly desired by Chinese emperors, who called them "blood-sweating horses" and sent expeditions with large amounts of gold to trade for them with the Teke tribe of Turkmenistan, where the breed originated.

The swift Akhal-Teke horses were originally bred for war and raiding, and they were naturally suited as racehorses. Their lineage was kept pure, and the fame of the breed spread in the ancient world. It was believed that the horses were anointed with divine grace and therefore worth a fortune. Long and lean, the breed is notable for the metallic sheen that highlights its fine, thin coat. As with many ancient breeds, however, it came near extinction in the twentieth century, and now only a few thousand individuals exist.

Recent scientific study of contemporary horses who appear to "sweat blood" revealed that the bleeding is caused by a parasite in local river water that the horses drink. At a certain point in the life cycle of the parasite, it breaks through the horses' skin and causes the bleeding. This bleeding also occurs in the region's donkeys and cattle, but not in people.

## Q Can Tennessee Walkers trot and canter?

A They can, but they rarely do. This versatile breed originated in central Tennessee in the 1800s, where it was bred to do farm work, pull the family wagon, and serve as a smooth-gaited riding horse. A number of different breeds contributed to the mix, including the Narragansett and Canadian Pacer, Standardbred, Thoroughbred, Morgan, and American Saddlebred. Tennessee Walkers are so named because their three natural gaits are the flat-foot walk, running walk, and canter.

FAST FACT At the running walk, which can cover 10 to 12 miles an hour, many Tennessee Walkers nod their heads in time with their strides; some even click their teeth in rhythm.

Refined yet athletic, the breed is known for its calm temperament and adaptable nature. Individuals can range from 14.3 to 17 hands and can be any color. They are used for show, pleasure, and trail riding. (See *What is a "Big Lick" horse?*, page 186.)

## Q What are some common pony breeds?

A Over the centuries and in many different locations, ponies have served as pack and draft animals, pulled elegant conveyances, and taught generations of children to ride. There are many registered breeds of ponies, some with fewer than 100 animals and others with thousands of animals registered worldwide. Some pony registries require not only certain physical characteristics, but character traits as well. Pony character is typically described as willing, hardworking, gentle, and easy to handle.

The **Shetland Pony** is the oldest breed of equine in the British Isles and probably the most popular pony breed worldwide. It originated on the harsh Shetland Islands off the north coast of Scotland, where crofters domesticated it to carry peat from the bogs to be used as fuel, and to carry seaweed up from the shore to be used as fertilizer. For many decades, it pulled coal carts in the depths of mines in both Britain and North America.

They are gentle and docile but extremely strong and sturdy. The original Shetland type, standing no more than 10.5 hands, is stocky and short-legged, with a shaggy coat and heavy mane and tail. Two somewhat taller and lighter varieties are recognized in North America.

The **Connemara Pony** originated on the rocky, desolate, mountainous coast of Ireland, and is that country's only native breed. Early Irish farmers often could afford only one pony, typically a mare that could both work and provide offspring to be sold. These ponies vary in color, are gentle and sure-footed, and are adaptable to any situation. Among the larger ponies, ranging from 13 to 15 hands, they are used in many equestrian sports.

The **Pony of the Americas (POA)** was created in the 1950s specifically as a breed for children to show, with adults allowed to show the animals only at halter or with a cart. The founding sire was an Appaloosa-colored colt who was the offspring of an Arab/Appaloosa mare crossed with a Shetland pony stallion. Eventually, crosses with other breeds were accepted within the limits of the breed's requirements.

Ranging in size from 11.2 to 14.2 hands, the POA must have Appaloosa spots that are visible from a distance of 40 feet (12.2 m) and must have mottled skin, another Appaloosa trait, somewhere on his body. These versatile ponies are popular show and pleasure mounts.

The **American Quarter Pony** is a relatively new breed with an open registry that encourages a muscular, well-balanced, and solidly built animal with collected action. The breed averages 13.2 hands, and larger individuals can easily carry an adult rider. They may be any solid color or may have pinto or Appaloosa patterns. They are reputed to be calm, versatile, and very responsive. Because of these qualities, they are popular mounts for children, and are used for pleasure riding and gymkhanas, as well as all types of Western competition.

*The Welsh Pony is one of many ancient pony breeds that are still popular today for pleasure riding and competing.*

## THE SWIMMING PONIES OF CHINCOTEAGUE

Made famous by Marguerite Henry's *Misty of Chincoteague*, Chincoteague ponies are descendants of feral horses who were deposited on or swam to Chincoteague and Assateague Islands, barrier islands off the Maryland and Virginia coast. These days, they wander in a refuge on Assateague Island, maintained in two distinct herds that are separated by a fence at the Maryland-Virginia line. The Maryland herd is managed by the National Park Service, which maintains a sustainable population through the use of long-term contraception delivered by dart.

The Virginia herd, owned by the Chincoteague Volunteer Fire Company, is the subject of the famed annual pony penning. Every July, the ponies are herded across the narrowest part of Assateague Channel at low tide and swum across to Chincoteague, where they are examined by veterinarians and then herded through town as a carnival celebrates the event. Larger foals are auctioned off to keep the herd at a sustainable 150 or so individuals, with proceeds supporting the fire company. The next day, the herd swims back.

**Welsh Ponies and Cobs** trace their origins to Wales before the Roman invasion in 43 CE. For more than 100 years, the breed has been classified into categories divided by size and type: Cob and Pony. The word "cob" means a small and solidly built horse, while the pony type is smaller and more refined. Intelligent and strong, both types make outstanding driving horses, but they are natural jumpers and also compete in dressage, English and Western pleasure, and other events.

## Q What good are miniature horses?

A Miniature horses are the size of a very small pony, no taller than 34 inches (86 cm). There are over 30 registries for miniature horses just within the English-speaking world, with some breed registries accepting slightly larger animals and others preferring pony characteristics, such as short, stout legs and an elongated torso. The

American Miniature Horse Association standard states that a miniature horse should look identical to a full-sized horse when seen in a photograph that has no background reference points to indicate its actual size.

While minis are not generally not used for riding, even by children, many people enjoy driving them singly, in pairs, and even in hitches. Miniature horses are friendly and like to interact with people. For this reason, they are often kept as companions, pets, or service animals for people with disabilities. Although it is tempting to see them as very large canines, they retain natural horse behavior and are healthier when allowed to live outdoors with proper shelter and space to exercise. Miniature horses are quite hardy and live an average of 25 to 35 years. (See *What is the largest breed of horse? The smallest?*, page 84, and *Thumbelina — Bigger than a Breadbox*, page 85.)

> **FAST FACT** **Miniature horses are not measured in hands from the withers to the ground, but in inches from the last hair at the base of the mane.**

*Miniature horses can't be ridden but they make excellent harness horses. They are shown in singles, pairs, and hitches of up to 10.*

# TRAINING HORSES

# If You Whisper,
# They Will Listen

The first person to approach a horse and catch it was also the first trainer. It is unnatural for a horse, a prey animal, to allow a potential predator to come near, let alone sit on its back. The story of our mastery over the horse spans the gamut from brutal methods of breaking an animal's spirit to the "horse whisperer" techniques that stem from a full understanding of equine nature. From Xenophon, the Greek master, to present-day trainers, the highest goal has been to better understand how various cues can be used to teach a horse to respond in a particular way.

## Q How do you break a horse?

**A** You don't. The term "breaking" was used when training was an unsophisticated and often brutal affair. Breaking horses often meant tying them to a post or blindfolding them until the saddle was on and the rider aboard. Once freed, the horse usually began bucking and was spurred or whipped into a state of exhaustion and hence a semblance of submission. Other methods included hobbling the horse (tying the front legs together) for hours on end or forcing its head to one side or the other and tying it to a saddle for long periods.

Breaking was intended to crush what was considered the horse's rebellious spirit and terrify the animal into submission and compliance. Today, most trainers realize that better results arise from a gradual process of positive education based on a relationship of trust and an understanding of equine nature.

## Q When can you start training a horse?

**A** Some training can begin shortly after birth, when a foal becomes accustomed to being touched by humans. In the first few months of life, a foal can be gently taught to wear a halter, to lead, and to stand quietly when being handled. Yearlings can safely be driven in long lines as part of their early training, but training under saddle with a rider aboard normally doesn't start until the horse is at least 2 years old to allow for leg bones, in particular the knees, to finish developing.

In the general training of a saddle horse, a good deal depends on the horse's conformation. A solidly

*A foal can be handled gently from birth and taught the basics of being haltered and led, but the best training for a foal is to have some other youngsters to play with and some older horses to teach it good equine manners.*

built Quarter Horse, for example, often can handle a rider's weight at an earlier age than can a small, light-boned Arabian or Saddlebred. Larger breeds that are slow to mature, such as drafts and warmbloods, are often not started in real work until they are 4 or 5 years old. Racing Thoroughbreds are an exception, receiving their early saddle training at about a year and a half. Many people blame this early training for later breakdowns because of early injury to bones and ligaments that are not yet fully developed.

## Q What is a horse whisperer?

A In days gone by, the term referred to people who traveled around the country, purporting to possess magical abilities to tame horses. They often claimed they could produce positive results merely from whispering in the horse's ear.

The phrase was first applied to an Irishman named Daniel Sullivan, who reportedly traveled about England in the 1800s rehabilitating intractable horses who had been abused or injured. He didn't share his secrets to success, but people observed that he stood in front of the horse and appeared to be whispering to him. Talking to a horse in a low, repetitive tone often has a calming effect on the animal, which has no doubt spread the use of the term.

Today, "horse whisperer" can apply to someone who has studied horses and learned their psychology. By knowing why a horse reacts as he does to certain stimuli, the handler can take appropriate steps to achieve a positive result. This can be accomplished, to a degree, by talking to the horse, but the utilization of body language is even more important.

A good trainer communicates with hands, eyes, and body. Actions as simple as dropping the eyes and relaxing the shoulders can signal to the horse that he is welcome to approach. A hard stare and rigid stance feels threatening and tells the horse to stay back.

## THE FIRST HORSE WHISPERER

Xenophon was a Greek philosopher, historian, soldier, and great horseman who lived from about 430 to 354 BCE. He was an early advocate of understanding horse psychology as an important part of training. Much of his wisdom serves as a basis for modern-day horse training, as in this example:

> The one best precept — the golden rule in dealing with a horse — is never to approach him angrily. Anger is so devoid of forethought that it will often drive a man to do things which in a calmer mood he will regret. Thus, when a horse is shy of any object and refuses to approach it, you must teach him that there is nothing to be alarmed at, particularly if he is a plucky animal; or, failing that, touch the formidable object yourself, and then gently lead the horse up to it. The opposite plan of forcing the frightened creature by blows only intensifies his fear, the horse mentally associating the pain he suffers at such a moment with the object of suspicion which he naturally regards as its cause.

## Q What is natural horsemanship?

A This approach is the opposite of attempting to break a horse. With natural horsemanship, the trainer seeks to understand the personality of each animal, treating him as an individual with a particular history. The trainer learns to read equine body language and seeks a training approach that allows a willing response instead of forced submission. The trainer establishes herself as a confident leader in this herd of two, achieving that position with a firm and consistent approach, never with cruelty or fear.

As the late trainer and horsemanTom Dorrance put it: "The thing you are trying to do is to get the horse to use his own mind. You are trying to present something and then let him figure out how to get there."

*Working in the smaller confines of a round pen enables this rider to use training sticks and body movement to guide his horse, which is not wearing a saddle or bridle.*

## Q What is a round pen used for?

A A round pen is a circular enclosure that can be utilized in various stages of horse training and teaching riders. The size varies, but at a minimum, the handler should be able to stand in the center with the horse traveling in a circle around her at a distance of 30 feet (9 m). Early in the training process, a round pen often is used in teaching the horse to respond to commands to turn and stop, both on the longe line and at liberty. (See *What's the difference between longeing and long lining?*, page 114.)

In the enclosed space, the handler can work with the horse closely or at a distance without having to rely on a line. Because the pen is round, the horse has no escape routes, such as corners, for avoiding cues. At the same time, the horse has plenty of room to move about and make decisions in response to the trainer's signals. Round pens are often used to create a situation in which the horse has the freedom to move away from the handler, but is encouraged to come closer as the handler establishes rapport and trust, a process known as "joining up."

Many trainers also ride horses in the round pen, either at the beginning stages of training or when working with a difficult animal. The circular structure makes it impossible for the horse to bolt off in a straight line and discourages bucking. Riding instructors may use a round pen with beginning riders so they can work in a smaller space and be closer to the student. (See *What is natural horsemanship?*, page 110.)

## Q Do horses understand what we say to them?

A They can't understand many specific words, but they can certainly decipher tone and inflection. An excited or nervous horse often can be calmed with soft-spoken words from its rider. A gentle tone and relaxed body language, not the actual words, provide the calming influence. A loud or angry voice, in contrast, can excite or upset a horse.

Horses often do learn to respond to specific verbal cues through repetition. For example, to train a horse to respond to the word "trot," the trainer utters the word each time the gait is desired. The word is accompanied with a physical stimulus, such as a cue with a whip from the ground or a squeeze of the legs when riding. Before long, the horse learns to respond to the word itself without the additional stimulus. In fact, many lesson horses make the association without specific training, and some pay more attention to the instructor's verbal commands than to the rider on their backs.

## Q Do horses react to their riders' emotions?

A Horses can sense when their riders are anxious or nervous, and they sometimes respond in kind by shying, jigging around, or ignoring cues. A horse looks to its rider for security and will be ill at ease when the rider is unsure or frightened. Conversely, a calm rider can ease a horse's fears in scary situations, while handlers who become impatient or angry usually make the horse more frightened and confused.

# Some Trainer Talk

IF YOU SPEND ANY TIME AROUND HORSE PEOPLE, you might hear some of these phrases.

Blowing up. When a horse suddenly begins bucking in vigorous fashion while being ridden.

Cold-backed. A horse who has a tendency to buck when first saddled.

Counterfeit or cheater. A horse who might begin a training session in a calm and leisurely fashion and then, without warning, begins bucking.

Crow hopping. A mild form of bucking during which the horse might come off the ground with all four feet, but without enough vigor to dislodge the rider.

Earing a horse down. Gripping an ear with one hand and twisting it downward to cause pain. The pain may result in the horse standing quietly for the moment, but is almost guaranteed to make him headshy.

Flagging a horse. A method of desensitizing the horse to touch. A cloth is fastened to the end of a flexible rod and the cloth is rubbed over all parts of the horse's body until he no longer reacts to the touch or sight of the waving fabric.

Handle. Training a horse to respond quickly to subtle cues with reins, legs, and body. Such a horse has a "good handle."

Sacking out. Similar to flagging, sacking out is the process of accustoming a horse to a variety of stimuli, often starting with a cloth sack or towel. Other items that horses should be introduced to include plastic bags, balloons, umbrellas, jackets, and raincoats — anything that might flap or swish.

Snubbing post. A heavy post planted deeply into ground for tying a horse and training him to stand. Tying him so that his head is close to the post is called "snubbing."

Turn on a nickel and give you some change. Ability of a horse to stand in one spot and spin in a tight circle.

Horses are keenly attuned to a rider's body language, just as a good rider becomes attuned to the horse's body language. Quick, jerky movements of the rider's hands or involuntary tightening of her legs can create apprehension on the part of the horse. When the rider grips the reins tightly, for example, and puts undue pressure on the horse's mouth, the animal is apt to become agitated because he senses that the rider is tense or upset.

## Q Do horses love us the way we love them?

**A** Horses don't experience emotion in the same way that humans do. With horses, a better word than "love" would be "respect." The horse is a social creature with a need to create a definite order in the herd, which, for domestic horses, includes humans. To gain respect, the trainer or rider must establish herself as a trusted leader without instilling fear in the horse.

A horse should be taught to respect his handler's space and not intrude. This means that when the handler leads a horse, the animal walks beside her without bumping into her. To achieve overall respect, the horse must be handled consistently and predictably, with a combination of firmness and kindness. Anger and harsh punishment have no place in horse training.

Although not expressing "love" in that way that people associate with dogs, many horses are friendly and people oriented. They seem to enjoy and even seek out human company and are able to form deep and lasting bonds with people they trust.

**FAST FACT** When working on the ground with a horse, its left side is called the "near" side, while the right is the "off" side.

## Q What's the difference between longeing and long lining?

**A** The word "longe" is derived from the French word *allonge*, which means "extension." It is pronounced "lunge" and sometimes spelled that way. To longe a horse means to have him move in a circle around the handler at the end of a line. "Free longeing" is done with the horse at liberty. (See *What is a round pen used for?*, page 111.)

*Longeing is a good way to train a young horse to accept a bit and learn to balance itself while moving on a circle without having to accommodate the weight of a rider.*

*Long lining introduces the horse to being driven, in preparation for wearing a harness and pulling a vehicle or farming equipment.*

The longe line is a flat, light canvas or synthetic line 30 to 35 feet long (9–11 m) that can be attached to a regular halter, a special longeing cavesson with a ring on the noseband, or a bridle (to the latter in a way that doesn't pull on the horse's mouth). The handler often also carries a long, lightweight whip as an aid to keep the horse moving forward. The idea is to create a triangle, the points being the horse's head, the line in the handler's hand, and the whip in the other hand.

Longeing is used for many purposes — training a young horse to respond to cues before he is able to carry a rider, continuing training with a more experienced horse, exercising a horse who needs physical rehabilitation, or warming up before a training session. Longeing is a very useful technique for teaching riders in a situation where they can focus on their seat and legs without having to worry about guiding the horse.

Long lining, or ground driving, is the practice of working a horse from the ground with driving lines attached to the bit and passed either through the stirrups of a saddle or through the side rings of a surcingle (a strap that passes around the horse's girth). The trainer walks behind and slightly to one side of the horse and guides him with the lines.

Long lining introduces horses to driving and pulling, and is used to train both carriage and plow horses. It is also an excellent training method for young horses who aren't mature enough to carry the weight of a rider. By the time they are ready for a rider, they are already responding to light squeezes on one or both lines, corresponding to reins.

## Q How are circus horses trained?

A Most circus horses perform at liberty, responding only to signals from the trainer. A lot of time and patience is required, as well as skill and understanding on the part of the trainer. It takes at least a year to properly train a horse for most acts, according to Yasmin Smart, granddaughter of legendary Billy Smart, a famous showman who created a traveling circus in England in 1946.

Yasmin began performing at age 7, riding horses, mules, zebras, and elephants. These days she performs with her own troupe of Arabian horses. She begins training a new equine recruit on the longe line, teaching the horse to respond to her body, voice, and hand signals. Eventually, a rider helps guide the horse through more complicated maneuvers. After learning the routine, the horse learns to respond to hand and voice signals alone and then begins working with other horses in the act.

## DON'T LEAVE ME BEHIND!

Sylvia Zerbini of Ringling Brothers Circus tells the story of a stallion who was retired at age 32. The horse was turned out into a lush pasture at Zerbini's Florida farm, but didn't take to his new life of leisure.

"We were on the road when I got a call from the farm," she said. "My helpers there said the horse was depressed and refused to eat. They were convinced he wanted to be back on the road. We drove 800 miles out of our way to pick him up and put him back in the show. When I loaded him into the van, backed him into his stall, and snapped the crossties, he started eating."

The old stallion remained a part of the show until finally accepting retirement two years later. Because of his age, he wasn't involved in strenuous activity, but participated in the opening segment and in parades.

One secret to success, Yasmin says, is to stop rehearsing once the horse learns the routine. Once trained, the only time her horses perform is when they are in front of an audience. And all of her horses receive treats at the end of each performance. Over time, she says, the horses become dedicated to performing well.

She tells of one performance where the horse on the outside of a pair was forced to jump out of the ring by the horse next to him. Instead of running off or panicking, the horse jumped back into the ring at the first opportunity and returned to his place in line.

## Q Why isn't the opposite of Western riding called "Eastern" riding?

A The two most common styles of riding, English and Western, each represent the culture in which it was developed. Western riding traces its roots to the vaqueros of Mexico and the cowboys of the Southwest and West, who spent many hours in the saddle tending livestock. The Western saddle is large and sturdy with a saddle horn. It is built up at the front and back to give the rider a secure seat during sudden stops and spins. It has to be strong enough to take the pull of a roped steer and comfortable enough for long rides during roundups.

The English saddle is much smaller and lighter, as it evolved from cavalry riding, where soldiers needed freedom of movement and the ability to move at speed. Modern versions were designed to accommodate riders who were hunting and jumping across England's countryside, pursuits that were formalized into competition such as three-day eventing and stadium jumping. English riding also encompasses dressage, saddle seat, equitation, and many other disciplines. In an English saddle, the rider has closer contact with the horse's body and relies more on balance to stay on board.

Here are some other differences:

**Reining**. An English rider holds one rein in each hand and uses direct reining, which means a slight pull on the left or right rein turns the horse to the appropriate direction. A Western rider holds the reins in one hand and uses neck reining — laying the rein against the horse's neck rather than pulling on the bit. Horses move away from pressure, so to turn left, the rider moves the right rein against the neck.

**Trot vs. jog**. An English trot and a Western jog are the same gait, but some of the early English horses had a rough trot that jolted the rider with each stride. To compensate, riders learned to rise out of the saddle on every other beat of the diagonal gait; this is called "posting" or "rising" to the trot. Western horses are bred and trained to have a smooth, slow jog and the Western rider either remains sitting in the saddle or stands in the stirrups for short periods.

**Canter vs. lope**. Again, these are different words for the same gait. At the canter, the English hunter rider angles her body slightly forward, balancing primarily on feet and thighs. That way, she is in position to go over a jump or remain balanced in the saddle for a long gallop. The Western rider, by contrast, sits down in the saddle so as to be in position for throwing a rope or making sudden turns when chasing cattle. Dressage riders also sit in the saddle during the canter, using longer stirrups than for English equitation to stay in contact with the horse's back and influence the gaits.

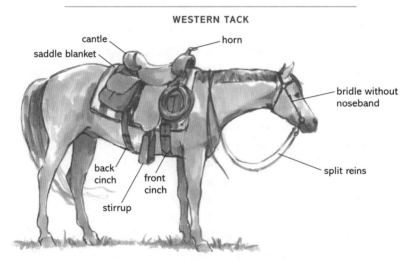

**ENGLISH TACK**

pommel

cantle

saddle pad

bridle with
noseband

closed reins

stirrup

girth

**WESTERN TACK**

cantle

horn

saddle blanket

bridle without
noseband

back
cinch

front
cinch

split reins

stirrup

# Q Why are there so many different kinds of bits?

**A** Although bits come in hundreds of styles, the main types are the snaffle and the curb. The snaffle bit has two cheekpieces and a jointed mouthpiece that puts pressure on the corners of the horse's mouth and on the tongue. The curb bit has shanks that extend downward from the cheekpieces. The mouthpiece can be either solid or jointed. It applies pressure on the toothless area of a horse's jaws, known as the bars.

The snaffle often is used in a horse's early training in an effort to keep him "light in the mouth." The bars, where the bit rests, are very sensitive, and applying undue pressure on them early in the training regimen can destroy this sensitivity. Once a horse is responding well to signals using the snaffle, some trainers, especially in the Western disciplines, often switch to the curb and seek improved responses with subtle pressure on the bars. Many horses, however, are ridden in snaffles throughout their lives.

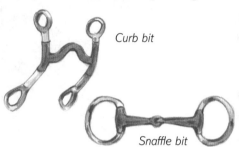

Curb bit

Snaffle bit

# Going Bitless

**MANY EARLY RIDERS** didn't use bits at all, instead training their horses to respond to leg signals and shifts in weight. Bitless headgear can range from a farm kid attaching rope reins to a halter, to more sophisticated devices designed to put pressure on the horse's nose, poll (the sensitive area just behind the ears), or cheeks rather than the bars and roof of the mouth. Some horses respond so well to bitless bridles that they are never introduced to the bit. Here are a couple of these devices.

A bosal is a bitless device developed by vaqueros in California for guiding and controlling a horse. It uses a combination of gentle pressure on the horse's nose and jawbones. The vaquero's horse was ridden in a bosal for up to three years before being introduced to the bit. The result was a soft-mouthed horse who responded to the lightest touch on the reins by the rider.

The mechanical hackamore features a strip or chain beneath the chin and a band over the nose. Both are connected to shanks on either side, with reins attached at the bottom of the shanks. This device can be cruel in the hands of an unskilled or unfeeling rider if the shanks are long, thus producing extreme leverage. The potential for pain is exacerbated when the nose and chin bands are tightened.

## Q What are the natural aids?

A The aids are how the rider communicates with her horse. The natural aids include a rider's seat, legs, and hands, in that order of importance. They are distinguished from the artificial aids, which are a crop or whip and spurs.

The seat refers to the rider's position and balance in the saddle; it encompasses the thigh and seat bones. The rider's weight in the saddle gives cues to the horse. For example, shifting your weight slightly forward often prepares the horse to increase its speed.

The legs in this case mean from the knee down. Horses move away from pressure and the legs are used in front of, at, or behind the girth to signal the horse to move forward or to turn. The legs can also signal a horse to stop turning or to stay straight.

The hands connect the rider to the horse through the reins and the ideal contact is light and elastic. The hands put pressure on one or both reins to facilitate turns or stops. An expert rider on a well-trained horse can ride without using the hands at all, relying on subtle shifts of seat and pressure from the legs to cue the horse.

FAST FACT **Some riders and their horses achieve such harmony that they can perform entire dressage or reining routines with no bridle at all, and in some cases, no saddle either.**

## Q What are direct, indirect, and neck reining?

A All three terms apply to guiding a horse while riding. The direct rein applies straight pressure on either the left or right rein to turn the horse in that direction. The indirect rein combines squeezing the rein toward the rider with rein pressure on that side of the neck. It often is used to position the horse's body, especially the shoulders, for certain movements.

Neck reining applies pressure on one side of the horse's neck. If rein pressure is applied on the left side of the neck, the horse will turn right or vice versa. Neck reining is mostly used in Western riding. (See *Why isn't the opposite of Western riding called "Eastern" riding?*, page 117)

## Q What does it mean to have soft hands?

A A rider with soft hands maintains proper contact with the horse's mouth through the reins without pulling or yanking. Maintaining light pressure on the bit with the correct rein length allows the rider to be in constant communication with the horse. Calm, steady hands instill confidence in the horse.

When a horse walks, his head nods up and down in rhythm with the four-beat gait. The rider with soft hands maintains light contact by moving her hands and elbows with the horse's head movement. When the horse trots, his head remains relatively stationary and the rider with soft hands holds the hands steady instead of bumping the horse in the mouth. When a horse canters or lopes, his head moves up and down, similar to the motion at the walk, and the rider's hands should mimic that motion.

## Q What does it mean to have a good seat?

A A good seat in the saddle means that the rider is balanced and her body is moving in synchrony with the horse. It all begins with proper posture. Seen in profile, an imaginary straight line down the rider's

*The correct posture in the saddle is often described as being one that would allow the rider to land on her feet if her horse suddenly disappeared out from under her. Note the straight lines running from shoulder to hip to heel and from elbow to wrist to the bit.*

side begins at the ear, goes down the shoulder and hip, and ends at her heel.

For the most part, her weight should be divided three ways, with some absorbed by her buttocks, some by her inner thighs and knees, and the remainder on the stirrups. From this position, the rider is able to respond to unexpected movement and remains in balance while she shifts her weight to signal to the horse.

**Q** What's the difference between a two-point seat and a three-point seat? Is there a one-point seat?

**A** In the three-point seat, the rider is balancing her weight on three points: her seat bones and both her feet. This position gives the rider security in the saddle and is the most common. When galloping or jumping, however, most riders rise slightly out of the saddle and balance their weight on their feet, leaving just two points of contact between them and the horse. The two-point, also called a "half seat," is less secure but gives the horse more freedom to move at speed. Riders who find themselves in a one-point position often wind up on the ground.

---

### LEFTWARD HO

Riders traditionally lead a horse and swing into the saddle from the left, a practice that traces back to the days when knights, and later cavalrymen, were armed with swords. The sword, encased in a scabbard, was typically carried on the rider's left hip, so the rider had to mount from the left in order not to become tangled with his weapon.

There is no other compelling reason to mount from the left, and all horses should learn to stand while the rider mounts from either side. It's good training for the rider as well, especially people who go out on trails and never know when and where they may need to dismount and remount. It is also better for the horse's back and for the saddle when a rider alternates the side from which she mounts, avoiding repeated stress on only one side.

---

## Q What is latent learning?

A With their excellent memories, horses retain knowledge even when not asked to use it for a period of time. Trainers may stop the training process for a few days or even weeks if they feel a horse has absorbed his maximum for the moment. After some time off, the horse is put back in training and, in most cases, not only demonstrates what he learned during the previous sessions, but proves that he has actually advanced mentally and emotionally in the time off and is ready for new challenges.

## Q When were saddles first used?

A We have evidence that saddles first came into use about 4,000 years ago. Before that, based on drawings, riders used little more than a patch of cloth or hide. As time went on, the cloths and hides became more elaborate. By 700 BCE Assyrian warriors rode on decorative cloths that often were held in place by a girth or strap around the horse's middle.

In the area that is now Siberia, the nomadic Scythians developed saddles that were both beautiful and functional. A Scythian saddle recovered from a fifth century tomb was intricately decorated with animal motifs made of leather, felt, hair, and gold. It was held in place by a girth. The Scythians may also have developed the first stirrups, although some historians believe that stirrups were first used by the warriors of Attila the Hun.

The precursor of today's Western saddle was developed by the Moors of North Africa. When they invaded Spain in the eighth century, they rode in saddles with high cantles (back) and pommels (front) to provide stability. The saddles were a carryover from those used by Crusaders who went into battle wearing armor. The Spanish adopted the Moorish saddle and it was introduced into the New World by armor-wearing conquistadors. It was modified by the vaqueros of Mexico when they began tending cattle, and further adapted by American cowboys.

The English saddle as we know it today was first designed for Hungarian cavalry, known as hussars, in the mid- to late 1400s. The hussars were more lightly armed and much more mobile than armor-clad combatants. They developed a hornless lightweight saddle that allowed freedom of movement during battle.

## Q How does a rider stay put in a sidesaddle?

A The earliest known type of sidesaddle, developed in the 1400s, was a stuffed pillow, known as a pillion, attached behind a man's saddle, hence the phrase "to ride pillion," which today can also refer to a motorcycle passenger. The lady, in her long skirts, was positioned sideways on the pillion. Later, a saddle was developed on which the lady rode her own horse with her right leg anchored between two horns for security. The left foot is in a stirrup, giving further stability.

The sidesaddle was perhaps most fully developed in England during the reign of Queen Victoria. The sidesaddle horse was trained to walk quietly and to canter in calm, collected fashion. He was not allowed to trot because it was thought unseemly for a lady to bounce up and down.

*According to the International Side Saddle Organization, "Ladies are currently riding aside in all disciplines, including, but not limited to, dressage, hunter/jumper, field hunting, English disciplines, Western riding disciplines, trail riding, reining, barrel racing and much, much more."*

# Straight Ahead in a Sidesaddle

SIDESADDLE ENTHUSIASTS like to point out that Sybil Ludington, a 16-year-old girl, was mounted sidesaddle when she rode through the night in 1777 to spread word of a British attack on a Connecticut town, much as Paul Revere and William Dawes had done two years earlier in Boston. They also point out that Sybil, unlike the men, didn't get caught.

Historical accounts of Sybil's ride vary, but it is known that Sybil's father was a colonel in the Patriot militia, living in what is now Kent, New York, where he operated a mill. A strong British force invaded Danbury, Connecticut, and captured storehouses filled with rebel supplies, including rum. The British soldiers consumed much of the rum and then went on a drunken rampage, burning and pillaging.

A rider from Danbury brought word of the attack to Colonel Ludington at 9:00 P.M. As members of the militia were scattered throughout the area at their homes, Sybil took on the task of alerting them, leaving home on a rainy night and riding a total of 40 miles (64 km) in the dark over rough and rocky roads and trails. Sybil roused the men in time to engage the British force in battle. They slowed the advance of the troops, but it was too late to save Danbury. A statue of Sybil riding sidesaddle on a charger is a featured attraction in Carmel, New York.

## Q When did spurs come into use?

A Spurs found in an Etruscan tomb date back to the second century BCE, before the establishment of the Roman Empire in Italy. Roman cavalrymen further developed the spur as a means of guiding their horses while leaving their hands free to handle weapons. Xenophon, writing in 365 BCE, discusses a rider being ready to "apply the spur" when teaching a horse to jump.

The original spurs had a single, sharp protrusion. The roweled spur was developed in the early 1200s CE by the French, who added a small revolving wheel or disk with radiating points attached to the shank. Spurs were introduced to the Americas by the conquistadors and were modified by vaqueros and cowboys. Today Western riders are more likely to use a version of a roweled spur than are English riders, who typically use ones with blunt points.

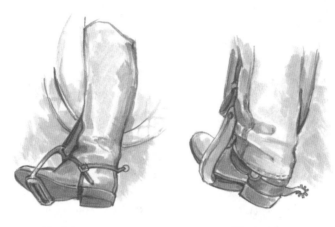

English spur                              Western spur

### EARNING ONE'S SPURS

In the days of knights and chivalry, spurs denoted rank. Gold or gilded spurs were worn by knights and royalty while the spurs of esquires were silver and those of valets were tin. Knights often vied with each other to own the most elaborate spurs in the realm, often encrusting them with jewels. Spurs were so highly valued that they were usually buried with the owner.

When a valet became an esquire or an esquire was knighted, the new status was commemorated with the fitting of new spurs for the honoree in a special ceremony; thus the expression "earning his spurs."

In the rare case when a knight disgraced himself, his sword was broken and his spurs were chopped off with a cleaver in a public ceremony.

## NEW YORK CITY CARRIAGE HORSES

Picturesque carriage rides through New York City's Central Park remain a popular tourist attraction and an occasional special event for locals. As of 2009, there were 203 licensed carriage horses in New York City, with almost 300 licensed drivers and 68 carriages pursuing this sometimes controversial line of work.

Fumes from cars and buses in the congested midtown streets, the noise level, and the possibility of extreme weather conditions make this a challenging life for a horse and driver. New York City carriage horses must be between 5 and 26 years of age. Rides in the streets outside the park are limited to nights and Sundays when traffic is light. The horses must have stalls that are large enough to turn around and lie down in, and they are entitled to 5 weeks off each year, which they spend at a stable with a paddock or a pasture turnout.

Regular inspections seek to enforce rules about sanitation and humane living and working conditions for the horses, but there are always concerns that some horses are overworked, neglected, or abused. The carriage drivers belong to the Teamster's Union, a group that was formed in 1903 by the drivers of teams of horses who delivered heavy freight.

## Q Who needs horses to do work these days?

A Although most horses today are recreational animals, many others do have serious jobs to perform. For example, ranchers ride horses to herd and handle cattle and sheep, as they have for centuries. Livestock must be gathered and moved, often over land that is too rugged for vehicles.

As interest in sustainable agriculture grows, draft horses are increasingly making a comeback on the farm scene. Some religious sects, such as the Amish, reject mechanized equipment and have always done all their farming with horses, as well as traveling by horse and buggy. Draft horses are still used in mountainous country and on sustainably managed woodlots to skid out logs and pull loads of lumber. (See *All-American Drafts*, page 86.)

Besides in agriculture, horses are used by law enforcement departments in many cities around the world, thousands of horses patiently work as lesson and school horses and provide mounts for young people at summer camps, others carry riders and their equipment into the mountains on camping trips. Some horses perform important duties in providing therapy for handicapped individuals. (See *How can riding be therapeutic?*, next question.)

And don't forget the fields of entertainment and sports: Many horses earn their keep in front of cameras or as circus or equine theater performers, and of course there are racehorses. (See chapter 6.)

## Q How can riding be therapeutic?

A The therapeutic use of horseback riding for people with physical disabilities can be traced back to the ancient Greeks, when Hippocrates mentioned it as "natural exercise." Equine-facilitated therapy programs benefit children and adults who have developmental, physical, cognitive, and emotional disabilities such as autism, cerebral palsy, or multiple sclerosis. Horses are also used therapeutically with combat veterans and others who have suffered physical or emotional trauma.

Participants and their families are extremely enthusiastic in their anecdotal reports of impressive gains, and supervised riding has grown increasingly popular as a therapeutic strategy to improve the rider's self-confidence and emotional well-being as well as physical, occupational, speech, and language skills.

On a physical level, riding a horse and adjusting to his motion improves posture, balance, and core strength in the abdomen, neck, back, and hips. It also loosens joints, stimulates muscles, and improves coordination. Because horses are temperamentally attuned to humans, riding and handling a horse in a safe environment provides a physical and emotional experience that fosters learning, trust, and a sense of responsibility.

On a cognitive level, riders learn skills that are necessary to affect the behavior of their horse, which can translate to success in other settings where they can make use of skills such as sequencing, focus, determination, and patience.

|| FAST FACT **Miniature horses have been successfully trained to act as assistance animals for blind and disabled handlers.**

## Q Can you train a horse to stand still without being tied up?

A Ground tying is important to ranchers and cowboys when they need to dismount in open country to repair a fence or carry out other tasks. A properly trained horse will stand without being attached to anything as long as the reins are dropped to the ground. The training process begins with tying the horse to an object so that he must remain on the spot. As training progresses, the trainer drops the reins to the ground and steps away from the horse, remaining close enough to grab the reins and give a verbal *whoa* if the horse seeks to move.

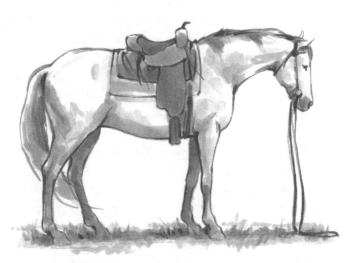

*Ground tying is primarily a Western technique used by ranchers and cowboys who spend a lot of time climbing on and off their horses and don't always have a place to tie them while they attend to livestock or fix a broken fence.*

## LEAP OF FAITH

While a horse has a field of vision of more than 350 degrees, he also has two cone-shaped blind spots (see *Do horses have good eyesight?*, page 37). One extends about 4 feet (about 1 m) immediately in front of him and the other 8 to 10 feet (2.4 to 3 m) directly behind.

When a horse is asked to jump over a fence, he loses sight of the jump just before he becomes airborne. Training a horse to jump begins over very low jumps with a pole on the ground in front of the jump as a sight line. The sight line helps the horse to determine the appropriate takeoff spot.

In addition, the horse must learn to have faith in his rider, who signals him when the takeoff spot is reached. A horse who is unsure of the takeoff spot or confused by his rider's signal may refuse to jump or miscalculate the approach. The result can be a spectacular and highly dangerous crash when fences are high, such as in Grand Prix jumping.

Eventually, the trainer steps farther and farther away for longer periods of time as the horse becomes habituated to remaining in one spot until being asked to move. The overall success rate, however, can be hit-and-miss. If something frightens the horse, he might jump back, realize he isn't really tied after all, and run off.

## Q Is it okay to feed horses treats like carrots and sugar?

A Feeding treats is something of a two-edged sword with horses. On the one hand, treats can be used carefully to reinforce desired behaviors and advance training in certain areas, particularly trick training. Many people enjoy offering treats to their horses after a good ride or as a way to show affection. On the other hand, some horses become pushy and demanding when regularly offered treats and might even nip or tear at clothing when one is not forthcoming.

Before offering anything to a strange horse, ask permission of the owner. Some people do not feed treats by hand at all, preferring to drop them in a feed bucket or on the ground. Treats given by hand should be offered on an outstretched palm, with fingers open and well out of the way. Horses cannot see what is going into their mouths, and can easily mistake a finger for a carrot.

As for health concerns, eating sugar cubes, peppermints, and other sweets has not been shown to lead to cavities the way it might for humans. When horses do develop cavities, it is generally as a result of some injury to a tooth or uneven wear and tear on the teeth. With regular dental care and good manners, there's no reason horses can't have treats. (See *Yes, We Do Eat Bananas*, page 42.)

## Q Why do some horses drool when being ridden?

A Having a bit in his mouth stimulates a horse's salivary glands, and if his head is relaxed, the saliva will flow freely, though usually not copiously. This prevents the bit from chafing the lips or tongue and, as a result, the horse is more responsive to light touches on the reins. If a tense or distressed horse is holding his head in an awkward position or clenching his jaw to avoid the bit, chances are his mouth will be dry. In that case, the bit can be irritating and even inflict pain.

In dressage, a horse with a moist mouth, demonstrated by a slight foam of saliva on the lips, is said to be "wearing lipstick." When the dressage horse's head is inappropriately pulled down to where his nose is well behind the vertical, however, the horse is unable to swallow and saliva flows out of his mouth. Excessive drooling is a sign that the horse is being improperly ridden.

## Q Can you clicker-train a horse?

A Clicker training, first developed for use with dolphins, is an approach used with many animals and can be quite successful with horses. A small clicker device is used to reinforce desired behaviors; because the sound of the click is initially "loaded" or associated with a treat or praise, it can eventually be used instead of an actual treat to shape a behavior, such as lifting a foot, or teach a trick, such as picking up a toy from the ground.

Once a horse knows that the click means "good job!" and is often followed by a reward, the trainer either solicits a particular behavior (pulling gently on a lead rope to lower the head, for example) or waits until the horse offers the desired behavior and then gives an immediate click. After a few attempts, the horse realizes that lowering his head is the desired behavior and the trainer can then add a cue or command (*head down*).

Intermittent rewards work better to reinforce desired behavior better than a constant stream of goodies. Eventually, the trainer "fades" the click as the command is solidly learned.

## THE ROYAL CANADIAN MOUNTED POLICE

Perhaps the most recognizable police officer in the world is a member of the Royal Canadian Mounted Police (RCMP), attired in a scarlet tunic, dark riding breeches with a yellow stripe down the side, and a broad-brimmed Stetson hat. Although horses are no longer used in regular police work, the RCMP maintains a breeding facility to produce the horses who still perform in the Musical Ride, an exhibition of equestrian skill that began in 1876, with public performances starting in 1904.

Thirty-two riders and a group leader, mounted on large black horses, execute a series of intricate maneuvers and cavalry drills choreographed to music. Each member of the group carries a long lance, with a pendant waving from the tip. The stirring climax to each performance involves a galloping "charge" the length of the arena with lances lowered.

The horses, bred for color, size (between 16 and 17 hands), and temperament, are a cross between Hanoverian and Thoroughbred. Riders who have been in the RCMP for at least two years can apply for a position in the Musical Ride. After performing with the Musical Ride for three years, they are rotated to other duties. The troupe performs throughout Canada as well as at international venues.

**CHAPTER SIX**

# HORSE RACING

# The Sport of Kings *and* Commoners

**I**t can't have been long after the horse was domesticated that two
riders started arguing about whose horse was the fastest. Historical
evidence shows that racing has been around in various forms for many
thousands of years. More recently, it has become highly specialized, with
some horses being bred to run short distances and others to compete
over longer courses; some to jump huge obstacles at full speed and
others to pull a lightweight cart at a flat-out trot. Whatever the venue, a
pack of horses racing neck and neck to the finish line is guaranteed to
stir the blood of spectators.

## Q How far back in history does horse racing go?

**A** Nomadic tribesmen of central Asia domesticated the horse about 4500 BCE and it is likely that racing in some form developed soon after. Among the first organized races were those conducted by the Greeks and Romans; both chariot races and mounted races were a part of the Olympics in 638 BCE.

The roots of modern horse racing trace back to the twelfth century when English knights returned from the Crusades with Arabian horses. These stallions and others were crossed on English mares, producing horses with both speed and endurance. Match races involving two horses became popular among English nobility; these gave way to contests that included several horses.

Henry VIII (r. 1509–1547) encouraged the breeding of light horses that were suitable for racing. The King decreed that "weedy" stallions be destroyed to prevent them from reproducing. He also established the Royal Studs — farms around England where quality horses were bred and raised. James I and Charles I continued the effort and racecourses sprang up in a number of locales.

During the reign of Charles II (1660–1685), horse racing became entrenched in English culture. The Jockey Club was formed in 1750 to establish rules and regulations for racing. The organization governs the sport in England to this day.

## Q What role does the Jockey Club play in North America?

**A** The Jockey Club is the breed registry for Thoroughbred horses in the United States, Canada, and Puerto Rico. Dedicated to the improvement of Thoroughbred breeding and racing, it serves many segments of the industry and supports a wide range of racing industry initiatives.

> *Horse sense is the thing a horse has that keeps it from betting on people.*
>
> — W. C. FIELDS

# Different Kinds of Races

People race horses all over the world and in all sorts of venues and types of competition. Contests in North America range from 250-yard (229 m) sprints to long distance endurance rides of 100 miles (161 km) or more.

Sprint racing. Generally contested by Quarter Horses over straight distances ranging from 250 to 440 yards (229–402 m), although some are longer.

Flat racing. Normally run over distances that range from three quarters of a mile to a mile and a half (1.2–2.4 km) around an oval track. Most flat racing is done by Thoroughbreds, but some breed organizations also hold races specifically for their breeds.

Steeplechase racing. Races of 2 miles (3.2 km) or more with the horses jumping over fences or other obstacles on the course.

Harness racing. A modern offshoot of chariot racing, these races are generally a mile (1.6 km) long. Most feature Standardbreds pulling sulkies, also known as racing bikes, while either trotting or pacing.

Endurance racing. Long-distance contests conducted at a moderate rate of speed, endurance races can be 100 miles (161 km) or more. Along the route, horses are periodically examined by veterinarians and must be declared healthy and capable of continuing the race. Arabians excel in this sport.

## Q Why is jumping over hedges called steeplechasing?

A British farmers and gentry tested the mettle of their hunters (horses used in foxhunting) by competing in races that traversed a general route across the countryside rather than a prescribed course. Riders had to negotiate whatever obstacles were in their path between starting and finishing points. The finishing point was a landmark that all the contestants could see, and because church steeples were frequently the most visible landmark, one often served as the finish line.

The first recorded steeplechase was held in County Cork, Ireland, in 1752. Steeplechase racing began in England at about the same time. Organized steeplechase racing debuted in about 1830 with established courses ranging from 2 to 4 miles (3.2–6.4 km) long and including various obstacles, such as stone walls, water jumps, brush fences, and timber rails.

The most famous steeplechase in the world is the Grand National held each year at Aintree, England. The course is 4 miles (6.4 km) long and the horses are required to jump 30 large, solid fences, many of them made of hedges, brush, and other natural materials. The race, although very popular in England, is controversial because of the danger of the course. In 162 runnings of the Grand National, 58 horses and one jockey have died.

A prominent steeplechase in America is the U.S. Grand National, held annually at Belmont Race Course in New York, where jumps are set up around the infield. Other prestigious steeplechases include the Carolina Cup in spring and the Colonial Cup in fall in South Carolina; the Maryland Hunt Cup in spring, and in Virginia, the Virginia Gold Cup Race each May and the International Gold Cup every fall.

> FAST FACT *National Velvet* by Enid Bagnold tells the story of Velvet Brown, a butcher's daughter from an English village, who wins a horse in a raffle and against all odds rides him to victory in the Grand National.

## Q How long are most Thoroughbred races?

A Early Thoroughbred races in England were a combination of speed and endurance, with many being run in 3- or 4-mile (4.8–6.4 km) heats (preliminary rounds), sometimes with no more than 15 minutes between races. A horse who won two heats was the race winner.

Over time, contests over shorter distances became more popular. Breeders concentrated on developing a longer-legged, more slender racehorse. Today, most Thoroughbred races are run at 1 mile (1.6 km) or less, with the longest ones in America being 1.5 miles (2.4 km). (See *How far back in history does horse racing go?*, page 135.)

## Q How many furlongs are in a typical race?

A A furlong is a measure of distance equal to one-eighth of a mile. In other units of measurement, it computes to 220 yards, 660 feet, or 201 meters. The term has been adopted by the racing fraternity to designate race distances under 1 mile (1.6 km); i.e., a 6-furlong race is three-quarters of a mile.

The word furlong is derived from the old English words *furh* (furrow) and *lang* (long). A 1-acre field was an eighth of a mile long.

> *The race is not always to the swift, nor the battle to the strong, but that's the way to bet.*
> — DAMON RUNYON

## Q What is the difference between a stakes race and a claiming race?

A A stakes race involves a stake or entry fee paid by the horse owner. Normally, the track adds an additional amount and the total becomes the prize money. Stakes races are graded 1, 2, and 3 by a committee of the Thoroughbred Owners and Breeders Association. A Grade 1 Stakes Race is the highest level and usually involves talented racehorses with winning records. Grades 2 and 3 are also for elite Thoroughbreds, but with less stringent criteria at each level.

A claiming race is one in which any entrant may be bought, or claimed, after the race for a set price, which is established before the race begins. The buyer files a claim for a particular horse with track officials before the race and becomes the owner of that horse on payment of the claiming price. Any prize money the horse wins in that race goes to the former owner.

## ECLIPSE FIRST AND THE REST NOWHERE

One of the most significant racehorses of all time was a stallion named Eclipse, so named because he was foaled in England on April 1, 1764, the date of a solar eclipse. Eclipse began his racing career at the age of 5 and ended it just 17 months later. After 19 wins in 19 races, few owners would run their horses against him because almost all of the bettors backed Eclipse. Co-owner Dennis O'Kelly is credited with coining the phrase "Eclipse first and the rest nowhere" as he placed a bet on the horse, who by some reports had the odd habit of running with his nose close to the ground.

Eclipse had an equally impressive career at stud, siring several hundred winners. It is estimated that somewhere between 80 and 90 percent of all modern Thoroughbreds have Eclipse's bloodline in their pedigrees. Eclipse died in 1789 at the age of 24 and his skeleton is housed at the Royal Veterinary College, Hertfordshire, England.

The most prestigious awards given in the American Thoroughbred racing world are the Eclipse Awards, which are presented by the National Thoroughbred Racing Association, Daily Racing Forum, and the National Turf Writers Association. The most coveted of these is Horse of the Year.

# Q Who was the fastest Thoroughbred racehorse ever?

**A** This question is impossible to answer satisfactorily because conditions change from track to track and overall track technology has improved over the decades. Also, the best racehorses of different eras are never able to race against one another, leaving dream matches to the imagination of the fans. But a few names consistently show up in lists of the greatest racehorses of all time, including Man o' War, Citation, Secretariat, and five-time (1960–64) Horse of the Year Kelso.

*One of the best racehorses in history, Secretariat won the 1973 Belmont Stakes in 2 minutes, 24 seconds, which computes to 38 mph (61 km/h) over a mile and a half (2.4 km). He finished 31 lengths ahead of his closest rival. That time has yet to be bettered in a race of that length.*

# On the Flip of a Coin

ONE OF THE MOST FAMOUS RACES in the world, the Epsom Derby, run at Epsom Downs in Surrey, England, was named on the flip of a coin. Legend has it that noted racehorse owner Lord Charles Bunbury was dining with his good friend, the Earl of Derby, when the discussion turned to naming the newly established race that would be run in spring 1780. Should it be "The Bunbury" or should it be "The Derby"? They flipped a coin for the honor, with the Earl of Derby winning. The word "derby" has come to mean any sort of race or other competitive endeavor. Ironically, the first Derby was won by Lord Bunbury's colt, Diomed.

Though now a prestigious racecourse, Epsom Downs originally had nothing to do with horse racing. A farmer named Henry Wicker is credited with discovering mineral-laden water in the hills in 1618 and residents of nearby London were soon flocking to the area, turning it into a popular spa with reputed healing powers.

The curative power of Epsom salt, which is composed primarily of magnesium and sulfur, is still touted today. Humans use it for a variety of maladies, ranging from rheumatism to digestive problems, and horse owners often use it for remedies, such as soaking an abscessed foot or applying a poultice to an injury.

## Q Who is the "Churchill" in Churchill Downs?

**A** Churchill Downs is named after John and Henry Churchill, who owned the land on what was then the outskirts of Louisville, Kentucky, where the track was constructed. The key figure in the development of this famous racetrack was Merriwether Clark, Jr., a nephew of the Churchills and a grandson of William Clark of Lewis and Clark Expedition fame.

In 1873 the Churchills leased the property to young Clark, who had traveled to Europe to learn more about racing and returned with a burning desire to establish a race patterned after the Epsom Derby in England. A famed socialite who loved to throw lavish dinner parties and drink expensive champagne, Clark built the track, which was a financial failure until the early 1900s.

> FAST FACT **Downs, as in Churchill Downs and Epsom Downs, comes from an old English word meaning "hills."**

## Q How many horses have won the Triple Crown?

**A** The Triple Crown is the American championship series for the best 3-year-olds in the sport. It comprises the Kentucky Derby, a 1.25-mile (2 km) race at Churchill Downs in Louisville, Kentucky, on the first weekend in May; the Preakness, a 1.06-mile (1.7 km) race at Pimlico Downs in Baltimore, Maryland, held 2 weeks later; and the 1.5-mile (2.4 km) race, the Belmont Stakes, at Belmont Park on Long Island, outside New York City, held 3 weeks after the Preakness.

As the horses enter the track at Churchill Downs on Derby day, the song "My Old Kentucky Home" brings people to their feet; at the Preakness, it is "My Maryland;" and at the Belmont Stakes, "New York, New York" announces the beginning of the race. The Derby is known as the "Run for the Roses" for the blanket of red roses draped around the winner's neck. At the Preakness, the garland is made of black-eyed Susans, and at the Belmont, the winner wears white carnations.

Only 11 horses have won the Triple Crown in more than 130 years of competition. They are:

- 1919 Sir Barton
- 1930 Gallant Fox
- 1935 Omaha
- 1937 War Admiral
- 1941 Whirlaway
- 1943 Count Fleet
- 1946 Assault
- 1948 Citation
- 1973 Secretariat
- 1977 Seattle Slew
- 1978 Affirmed

**FAST FACT** **A horse might win a race by a neck, a nose, or even just a whisker, giving the fans an exciting show. Or he might win by a length or more, meaning he is ahead by at least the body length of an average horse (about 9 feet from nose to tail).**

## NO REGRETS

When the first filly to win the Kentucky Derby was born in New Jersey in 1912, she was named Regret because her owners were sorry that she was not a colt. But in her very first race as a 2-year-old running against colts, she won by a full length over the favorite. Before the year ended, she had won three stakes races.

Contrary to normal practice where Derby-bound horses race in 3-year-old prep races, Regret's first start at 3 was in the 1915 Kentucky Derby. The filly who had already been dubbed "The Legend of the East" lived up to her reputation by leading the pack from start to finish.

Regret won nine of the eleven races she ran. It was 65 years before another filly, Genuine Risk, won the Kentucky Derby in 1980, with only one other doing it since then — Winning Colors in 1988.

*The horse I bet on was so slow the jockey kept a diary of the trip.*

— HENNY YOUNGMAN

## Q When do you have a rabbit in a horse race?

**A** Trainers who have a "closer" or "come-from-behind horse," one who runs at a rather leisurely pace until accelerating in the home stretch, often enter another horse in the same race who tends to run very fast for at least part of the distance. The idea is for the fast horse — the rabbit — to set a pace that the other horses will try to match, presumably tiring as they approach the finish line. When the rabbit starts to fade, the closer, who has been running at the back of the pack, speeds up and passes the flagging pack.

Sometimes the strategy works and sometimes it doesn't. And sometimes the rabbit pulls a win out of his hat. A case in point is Aristides, the little horse who won the first Kentucky Derby in 1875. His owner, H. P. McGrath, who also owned the Derby favorite, Chesapeake, entered both horses in the Derby, with instructions that Aristides be the rabbit. Aristides shot out of the gate as planned and took the lead. Instead of fading, he maintained the pace and finished a length ahead of the field. Chesapeake finished eighth.

*Sometimes the "rabbit" upsets the trainer's plans and actually wins the race.*

HORSE RACING

## AFRICAN-AMERICAN JOCKEYS

In the early history of racing in America, many jockeys and trainers were African-American. In the first Kentucky Derby in 1875, 13 of the 15 jockeys were African-American, including Oliver Lewis, who rode winner Aristides (see *When do you have a rabbit in a horse race?*, facing page). The trainer of Aristides was Ansel Williamson, an African-American who was later inducted into racing's Hall of Fame. Fifteen of the first 28 Kentucky Derby winners were ridden by African-Americans and five were trained by African-American trainers.

One of the most famous jockeys was Isaac Murphy, who won 44 percent of all races in which he rode, including three Kentucky Derbies. His career was cut short when he died of pneumonia at the age of 34. He was the first jockey to be inducted into the Jockey Hall of Fame at the National Museum of Racing and Hall of Fame. Murphy is buried next to Man O' War at the Kentucky Horse Park.

Things changed at the turn of the century as racing became a high-profile sport. African-Americans were relegated to stable chores as racial prejudice took its toll and white jockeys took their place in the saddle. The last African-American jockey to win the Kentucky Derby was Jimmy Wakefield, winning in both 1901 and 1902. He moved his tack to Europe and rode more than 2,300 winners in his overall career before retiring. Today, although still in the minority at the track, African-Americans are again making their presence felt as owners, trainers, and jockeys.

## Q What does it mean when a horse places or shows in a race?

A Track-goers often hedge their bets by placing money on a horse to win, place (come in second), or show (come in third). Any of those results will return money to the bettor. The rest of the pack, or "also-rans," are "out of the money."

# Racing Lingo

**"MY HORSE WENT SIX IN NINE** and change and won it in a picture." If you heard that sentence at the races, would you have any idea what was being said? The translation is, "I entered my horse in a six-furlong race. He ran the distance in 1 minute, 9 seconds and a fraction. The race ended in a photo finish and the photo showed that my horse was the winner."

Here are some other racing terms to help you feel at home on the track:

**Across the board.** Betting the horse to win, place, and show. If the horse wins, you receive three payoffs. If the horse places, the payoff is for second and third, and if he shows, the payoff is for third place only.

**Allowance race.** A race where the weight to be carried by a horse is based on past performance.

**Also-ran.** Horses who finish lower than first, second, or third.

**Backside.** The area at a racecourse where the horses are stabled, also known as the shedrow.

**Backstretch.** The straight area of the track between the two turns.

**Bleeder.** A horse with a condition that causes bleeding in the respiratory system, which can compromise its ability to breathe when running.

**Blowout.** A short, very fast workout, usually a day or two before a race.

**Breeze.** Working a racehorse at moderate speed.

**Bug boy.** An apprentice jockey.

**Daily double.** Usually the first and second races of the day; to receive a payoff, you must correctly bet the winners in each race.

**Dark horse.** A horse who seemingly comes out of nowhere to win because he doesn't have the credentials to be a favorite.

**Dead heat.** When two horses finish a race so close together that even a photo finish can't determine a winner; the owners split the prize money, whatever the place.

**Distaff race.** A race for female horses only.

**Distance.** When a racehorse wins by 30 lengths or more, it is said to have won by a distance.

**Field.** The number of horses competing in a specific race.

**Going away.** When a horse wins a race and is lengthening the lead as he crosses the finish line he is said to "win going away."

**Handicapper.** Someone who rates horses as to their chances of winning. Every bettor at the track is a handicapper of sorts.

**Hardboot.** Originally the term was applied to Kentucky horse people in general, but now it refers to veteran race trainers.

**Homestretch.** The straight area between the final turn and the finish line.

**Hot walker.** A person who leads a horse to cool it off after exercising or racing.

**Lightning in a bottle.** When someone buys a horse for a small sum because his potential is deemed to be limited and the horse goes on to be highly successful, the buyer is said to have "caught lightning in a bottle."

**Maiden.** A horse who hasn't won a race. When it wins its first race, it is said to "break its maiden." Some races are for maidens only.

**Mudder.** A horse who prefers to run on a wet or muddy track.

**Odds-on.** When betting odds on a horse are less than even.

**On the nose.** Betting a horse to win only.

**Parimutuel betting.** All the money that is bet is divided among the winning bettors after the track has deducted its designated share.

**Purse.** The money distributed to owners in a given race.

**Quinella.** A bet in which you select two horses to finish first and second; it doesn't matter what order they finish in.

**Racing plates.** Lightweight shoes, typically made of aluminum, that are fitted to the horse's hooves for each race. Different styles are available for different track conditions

**Router.** A horse who runs a given distance at a consistent speed.

**Sitting chilly.** When the jockey sits quietly on his horse without using the whip or undue body motion, especially as they near the finish line.

**Spit the bit.** A horse who seemingly gives up and slows down in a race.

**Stalker.** A horse who stays close to the front runners in preparation for making a move in the homestretch.

**Stretch call.** The position of field with 1 furlong remaining.

**Tout.** A person who advises bettors, often receiving money in return.

**Turn of foot.** A horse who accelerates quickly has "good turn of foot."

**Wire.** The finish line; a close race is one that comes "down to the wire."

**Work.** An exercise run during a training session that is timed by clockers, with the time attached to the horse's record of past performances.

## Q Are horses tested for illegal drugs the same way human athletes are?

**A** After a race, either urine or blood samples, or both, are collected and analyzed for illegal drugs by a laboratory that has been approved by the racing jurisdiction. When a race ends, designated horses must go to the test barn where urine is collected for drug analysis. The test stall is called the spit box, harking back to earlier times when the only drug tests were for cocaine or heroin in the horse's saliva.

The test stall is deeply bedded with fresh straw, which stimulates the horse to urinate. An attendant, armed with a cup attached to the end of a long stick, waits quietly in a corner of the stall and when the horse begins to urinate, captures some of it in the cup for analysis.

*Nobody has ever bet enough on a winning horse.*
— RICHARD SASULY

## Q Do racehorses have ID cards?

**A** Racehorses must have registration papers to run, but most also have a number tattooed on the upper lip. It is applied before the horse's first race. The practice was inaugurated for Thoroughbreds in 1947 and is now widely accepted among all racehorses. On race day, a track official checks the lip tattoos of all entrants against the identification number listed on the registration papers to ensure that a ringer (an imposter) is not being entered.

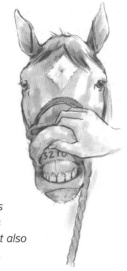

*The tattoo consists of a letter that indicates the horse's year of birth while the numbers constitute a unique registration number that also is affixed to the horse's registration papers.*

**Q** What's the difference between trotting and pacing?

**A** Both of these gaits are seen in harness racing, but there is a distinct difference. When a horse trots, his legs move in diagonal pairs: left front and right rear, right front and left rear. When he paces, his legs move in lateral pairs: left front and left rear and right front and right rear. There is little crossover between the two: trotters trot and pacers pace.

According to the U.S. Trotting Association, pacers generally come in about three seconds faster than trotters of comparable quality in a one-mile race. Race times for both gaits have dropped through the years with improvements in track surfaces and equipment. The fastest time in a race for a pacer to date is 1:46.4, recorded by Cambest in 2008. The fastest time for a trotter is 1:49.3, recorded in 2008 by Enough Talk.

*The pace, left, is a lateral gait, whereas the trot, right, is a diagonal one.*

Between 80 and 90 percent of Standardbred races in North America are for pacers, while in continental Europe, only trotters are allowed to compete. Both trotters and pacers compete in Canada, Australia, New Zealand, and the United Kingdom. In all harness races, the horses must maintain the gait without breaking into a gallop.

FAST FACT
**Old-time horsemen used to call pacing horses "side-wheelers."**

## THE BEST OF THE BEST

One of the greatest trotting horses of all time was a gray gelding named Greyhound, foaled in 1932. He won the Hambletonian as a 3-year-old and, in 1938, he lowered the record time for trotting the mile to 1:55.25, a mark that stood until 1969. At one time, Greyhound, affectionately called The Gray Ghost by racing fans, held 14 world records. He was retired in 1940 and lived out his days at Red Gate Farm in St. Charles, Illinois, where fans came from far and wide to see him. He died in 1965 at the age of 33.

In Standardbred circles, pacer Dan Patch is considered by many to be the greatest harness horse of all time. He was foaled in April 1896 in Indiana. In 1906, racing against time in front of a crowd of 93,000 at the Minnesota State Fair, Dan Patch set a world record for pacers of 1:55. He almost broke his own record in 1908. He was two seconds ahead of the pace set at Minnesota when he was bumped by the pacesetter, slowing him down. Dan Patch, who traveled to races and exhibitions in his own railroad car, died in 1916. His owner, Marion Savage, with whom the horse had developed a great bond, died 24 hours later.

## Q What are the most common injuries suffered by racehorses?

**A** The majority of injuries involve the front legs because a horse carries approximately 65 percent of its weight on the front limbs. At the gallop, there is a point in every stride where the horse's entire weight is transferred to one front leg. This tremendous concussive force can break bones and tear tendons.

Some race injuries are relatively mild and the horse recovers to race another day. Catastrophic ones usually result in the horse having to be euthanized.

**FAST FACT** An asterisk (*) on registration papers or racing sheets indicates that the horse was imported.

*In the world of mules, there are no rules.*

— OGDEN NASH

## Q Do mules race?

**A** Mule racing is very popular in parts of the United States, particularly California, where more than $2.5 million is wagered on 100 or more mule races during a typical season. A major impetus for mule racing came in 1995, when California approved parimutuel wagering on mule races. Mule racing is governed by the American Racing Mule Association, which was organized in 1976.

Mule races are patterned after Quarter Horse contests, with distances typically ranging from 350 to 400 yards (320–366 m). Mules aren't quite as fast as Quarter Horses, but their times are respectable, with winners covering 350 yards (320 m) in 20-plus seconds.

Mules must be 3 years old before they are allowed to race, and must retire after their 16th year. The American mule racing season opens in June in Winnemucca, Nevada, and then moves to California, where races are held at fairs throughout the state during summer and early fall.

## CLONED TO WIN

The first equine to be cloned was a mule named Idaho Gem, born in 2003. The cloning took place at the University of Idaho, with much of the cost being underwritten by mule racing aficionado Don Jacklin, a wealthy Idaho businessman who at the time was president of the American Racing Mule Association. The cells used in the cloning were from one of Jacklin's racing mules.

Subsequently, two other mules were cloned from the same genetics, making for triplets. Idaho Gem and another of the triplets, Idaho Star, made their racing debuts in 2006 in Winnemucca, Nevada. Idaho Gem finished third and Idaho Star seventh in a 350-yard (320 m) championship race. Idaho Gem won his first race later that year in Stockton, California.

Jacklin, who first leased and then purchased Idaho Gem from the University of Idaho, retired him from racing in 2008. (See *Can you clone a horse?*, page 9.)

## Q What is a Mongolian horse race?

A Racing is a significant part of Mongolian culture, with the most important races being held during Naadam, an annual festival that celebrates "the three games of men": horse racing, wrestling, and archery. (Today, girls can serve as jockeys in horse races and women compete in archery, but not wrestling.)

Hundreds of horses, ridden by children from 5 to 13 years old, compete in the races. The length of each race is determined by the horse's age. Two-year-olds, for example, race for 10 miles (16.1 km), while 7-year-olds race for 17 miles (27 km). Up to 1,000 horses from all over the country compete at the various festivals. The premier festival is held in Ulaanbaatar, the Mongolian capital, for three days in early July.

The competing horses are small but tough Mongolian horses who strongly resemble the little steeds that Genghis Khan and his warriors rode on their raids. They are trained and conditioned for months before the race to make sure they are extremely fit.

# Q What is the Tevis Cup?

A This 100-mile (161 km) endurance race from Nevada to California is also known as the Western States Trail Ride. The first Tevis Cup was awarded in 1959. Making the presentation to the winner was Will Tevis, the "Iron Man of the Age," so called because in 1923 he outlasted nine U.S. cavalrymen on a 257-mile (414 km) ride from San Mateo, California, to the Nevada border. Tevis switched horses during that celebrated ride, but took no rest for himself from start to finish.

The ride that now bears the Tevis name was started in 1955 by Wendell Robie, a prominent figure in Auburn, California, who declared that riders could cover the distance through rugged terrain in under 24 hours. Many scoffed at his assertion, so Robie and four other men proved his point by riding from Tahoe City, Nevada, to Auburn, California, in 22 hours and 45 minutes.

The ride has continued on an annual basis since that time. Robie finished first in the first four rides held and continued competing until well into his 70s. (See also *How can trail riding be competitive?*, page 157.)

# Q What is a Ride-and-Tie Race?

A This unusual endurance contest features teams of two humans and one horse who compete over courses ranging from 20 to 100 miles (32–161 km). Both members of the team start at the same time, one on the horse and one on foot. The mounted rider covers as much distance as she feels her fellow competitor can run. At that point she halts, ties the horse to a stout tree, and begins running. When the first runner reaches the horse, she mounts up and heads down the trail, passing the second runner and continuing on for what she considers to be an appropriate running distance for her companion.

This leapfrog approach continues until the end of the race. Midway through the race, there is a mandatory inspection of the horses by veterinarians. A team does not have to finish together, but its time is not recorded until both humans and the horse are across the finish line. Ride-and-tie contests began in 1971, and the sport has a national organization, the Ride and Tie Association.

## Q What was the longest horse race ever held?

A One of the longest, if not *the* longest, was held in 1976 from Frankfort, New York, to Sacramento, California, a distance of 3,200 miles (5,150 km). Dubbed the Great American Horse Race, each participant paid an entry fee of $500 and was allowed to lead a second mount as a backup. First prize was $25,000, with an additional $25,000 for the next nine finishers. There were 91 entrants and each had his or her support group, swelling the overall contingent to about 450 people. The race began on Memorial Day, May 31, and ended on Labor Day, September 6.

The winner was a 60-year-old steeplejack from San Jose, California, named Virl Norton, who traveled with two mules. His lead mule was a john (male) named Lord Vauntleroy, and his backup mount was a molly (female) named Lady Eloise, both out of Thoroughbred mares by a mammoth jack. Both mules were dark brown and stood 16 hands high. Norton and his mules covered the distance in 98 days and finished nine hours and 17 minutes ahead of the second-place entry. Fifty-four entrants finished the race.

When the race ended and some of the competitors complained about the way the race was run, Norton is quoted as saying: "Okay, give me 72 hours and we'll turn around and race back. We'll each put up $10,000, winner takes all." There were no takers. (See *A Lot of Time in the Saddle*, page 158.)

## Q What is the most money ever paid for a racehorse?

A The record was $16 million for The Green Monkey in 2006. The horse was a 2-year-old in training, sold at the Fasig-Tipton Calder Sale in Florida. The Green Monkey, sired by Forestry, is the descendant of three Kentucky Derby winners (Unbridled, Secretariat, and Northern Dancer). During the time trials before the sale, The Green Monkey ran an eighth of a mile (201 m) in under 10 seconds, the fastest time among more than 150 racehorses being offered.

He did not live up to expectations, failing to break his maiden (win a race) in three tries. He was retired in 2008 and stood at stud for the first time in 2009.

*Prime racing stock can sell for hundreds of thousands of dollars at auctions, even before running in a single race.*

## YOU GOTTA HAVE HEART

Great racehorses are said to "have heart," which refers to their courage and unrelenting determination to win. A number of equine researchers also believe that the size of a horse's heart has a bearing on how fast he can run. The heart of an average Thoroughbred weighs 8.5 pounds (3.9 kg). Triple Crown winner Secretariat, however, had a heart that was estimated to weigh 22 pounds (10 kg). (See *Who was the fastest Thoroughbred racehorse ever?*, page 140.)

Sham, the horse who competed against Secretariat in the Triple Crown races, was autopsied after his death at the age of 23. His heart weighed 18 pounds (8 kg). The heart of the great Australian racehorse, Phar Lap, weighed 14 pounds (6.4 kg).

# CHAPTER SEVEN

# PIAFFES, PULLING, AND POLO

## More Equestrian Sports

R ecreation on horseback can range from a peaceful walk along a trail to galloping headlong at an opponent in a jousting match. Games on horseback have existed for many centuries, some for pure sport (foxhunting), some as an extension of work (rodeo events), and some as training for war (jousting). Polo, now a glamour sport for the wealthy set, originated in Persia and was adopted by British officers stationed in India. Horse lovers have figured out ways to combine riding with other sports as varied as skiing, gymnastics, and basketball. Different breeds excel at different activities, but the horse is a versatile animal that often seems to enjoy the spirit of competition as much as its rider.

# Q Is trail riding a sport?

A It can be (see next question), but this popular equestrian pastime is mostly enjoyed by individuals or groups who meander along trails, explore the countryside, or go camping on horseback. A trail ride might involve a couple of friends trotting along a country road or it could be an organized affair with hundreds of people gathering for several days of riding. Most organized rides are much smaller, but the goal is always the same: to enjoy one's horse and the companionship of like-minded people.

A good trail horse is calm, willing, and comfortable to ride. Training a horse for the trail involves introducing him to a variety of obstacles and situations so that he learns to accept strange objects and new experiences.

> FAST FACT A horse that is overtrained in an arena might become "ring sour," whereas one that fusses about being separated from a companion is called "buddy sour." A horse that refuses to leave the stable willingly is known as "barn sour."

# Q How can trail riding be competitive?

A Some people take trail riding to the next level (or two) by turning it into a competition. Competitive trail riders travel a set distance over a prescribed route with various obstacles to be surmounted along the way. The contest is not a race, although all riders must finish within a set time.

Each team starts with 100 points, with points lost for faults in condition and soundness of the horse, manners, horsemanship, and performance. The horses undergo periodic vet checks and must meet certain fitness standards before riding on. Competitive trail rides can be as short as 10 miles (16 km) and as long as 100 (160 km).

Endurance racing notches up the competition by awarding the win to the team that completes the course, often over grueling terrain, in the best shape. Although speed is a factor — there is a time limit for finishing — the winning team isn't necessarily the one that finishes first. As with competitive trail riding, the focus is on fitness

*The national competitive trail record was set in 2008 by a 36-year-old half-Arabian gelding named Elmer Bandit. He and his lifelong owner, Mary Anna Wood, logged over 20,000 miles together. Elmer was healthy and active for two years after claiming the record and enjoyed his favorite treat of apples right up to the end.*

## A LOT OF TIME IN THE SADDLE

As young boys, brothers Bud and Temple Abernathy from Oklahoma made several amazingly long rides in the early 1900s, starting with a 1,000-mile round trip between Oklahoma City and Santa Fe when they were just 5 and 9 years old. In 1910 they rode to New York City, where they met Orville Wright, President Taft, and Teddy Roosevelt. The following year, now aged 7 and 11, they trekked from New York to San Francisco, arriving in just 62 days. They managed all three trips with parental permission, though not supervision.

Many other people have saddled up and hit the trail for months on end. One of the most famous was Aime Tschiffley, who started off from Buenos Aires in 1925 and made it to Washington, D.C. with his two Argentinian Criollo horses, Mancha and Gato. His fascinating book about his 3-year, 10,000-mile journey, *Tschiffley's Ride*, is out of print but readily available.

and conditioning, and horses must stop for breaks and pass through veterinary checkpoints every 10 to 15 miles. Horses that do not meet the checkpoint criteria are eliminated.

|| FAST FACT **The Long Riders' Guild is a fellowship of riders who are dedicated to traveling the world on horseback.**

## Q Do people still hunt foxes on horseback?

A Not in England, where chasing any quarry with hounds has been banned since 2005. Foxhunting remains popular in the United States, Canada, and a number of other countries, though in many locales, drag hunting has gained popularity as a substitute.

To prepare for a drag hunt, a dragsman puts down a scent trail, or dragline, by dragging along the ground a bag that contains animal droppings, urine, or aniseed along with paraffin or another fixative that prevents the scent from evaporating. The dragline usually winds back and forth across the countryside and includes jumps over fences and walls. The dragsman often attempts to imitate the antics of a live fox by putting scent along the top of a stone wall, doubling back, and circling about.

The dragline is established about half an hour before the hunt begins, and then the hounds are let loose and riders take to the field to follow them. The hunt ends when the hounds reach the end of the dragline where they receive treats and high praise for their work and the hunters celebrate with a libation of choice.

*Foxhunting is the unspeakable in pursuit of the inedible.*
— OSCAR WILDE

## Q Why do some foxhunters wear red jackets?

A Red jackets are worn by hunt officials, such as the Master of Hounds, huntsman, and whippers-in. The color is a mark of honor; red jackets are worn by former masters as well as individuals who have been invited by the hunt to wear red. Other members of the hunt normally wear a black coat.

# Tally ho! and Other Words to Hunt By

**Away.** A call signifying that the hounds have found the scent and are following it.

**Cast.** To send the hounds in search of the scent.

**Covert.** A wooded or brushy area where a fox might take refuge.

**Cry.** The voice of the hounds when they are on scent. As the hounds close in on their quarry and the sound increases in intensity, the hounds are said to be in "full cry."

**Cubbing.** The testing of young hounds during hunts before the formal hunting season.

**Drag hunt.** A hunt where the hounds follow an artificial scent trail rather than seeking out a live fox.

**Field.** The riders participating in the hunt, not including the hunt staff.

**Huntsman.** The person in charge of the hounds during the hunt itself. The huntsman normally carries a horn to communicate instructions to the hounds.

**Line.** In a drag hunt, the trail of scent for the dogs to follow.

**Master of Fox Hounds.** The person in charge of the kennels and the hunt; the ultimate authority in the field.

**Quarry.** The animal being pursued during a hunt.

**Ratcatcher.** Informal dress worn during cubbing, before the formal hunt season. It generally includes a black, brown, or gray tweed coat; tan, buff, or brown breeches; black or brown boots; and a white shirt with white stock.

**Riot.** When hounds leave the scent to chase other game.

**Run.** A gallop for the field when the hounds are hot on the scent of their quarry.

**Stirrup cup.** A toast, usually involving alcohol, given at the beginning or end of a foxhunt.

**Tally ho.** A shout to draw attention to something, such as sighting the quarry.

**Whippers-in.** Assistants to the huntsman whose job it is to keep the pack together and to prevent them from straying off after other game.

**Yoicks.** A cry of encouragement to the hounds.

## Q What other kinds of animals are hunted on horseback?

A In some parts of the United States where fox are scarce, a foxhunt becomes a coyote hunt. Coyotes are prevalent in most states and a number of hunts focus on them as quarry.

In other parts of the country, mounted hunters follow bird dogs in field trials, often accompanied by a crowd of spectators also on horseback. In the trials, the dogs, mostly pointers and setters, must locate as many birds (often quail or pheasant) as possible in a given time frame. In many cases, the birds are not shot, just counted.

In some European and South American countries, the quarry is an antlered male red deer. Hounds chase the stag until it is in position to be dispatched with a gunshot by hunters following on horseback.

## Q What breeds of horses are the best jumpers?

A Many breeds jump well and can be seen competing at lower levels. Ponies are often willing and talented jumpers, who help young riders begin their show careers.

At the upper levels, however, with the highest being Grand Prix jumping, Thoroughbreds and warmbloods tend to dominate the field. Warmbloods are horses who might carry the blood of draft horses, Thoroughbreds, Arabians, and other breeds. Breeders in many countries have developed national warmblood breeds.

In France, for example, the Selle Francais is a popular show jumper. During the 2002 World Equestrian Games, the entire French show jumping team, which won five of seven possible championships, was mounted on Selle Francais stallions. Germany, Holland, Sweden, and Denmark, among other countries, also are home to specific warmblood breeds. These equine athletes are also referred to as "sport horses." (See *What do you get if you cross a hot-blooded horse with a cold-blooded one?*, page 85.)

*Warmblood breeds are commonly seen competing at the top levels of show jumping and eventing.*

# Types of Jumps

**THE JUMPS USED IN STADIUM COMPETITION** are straight or vertical fences and spread (wide) fences. The degree of difficulty is determined by height, width, construction, and placement.

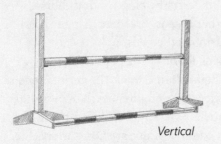

*Vertical*

**Vertical.** A straight-up-and-down fence without spread (width), this is one of the more difficult jumps for a horse because there is no baseline or sight line on which to focus.

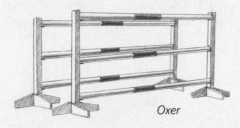

*Oxer*

**Oxer.** A jump consisting of two elements in one jump to produce a spread, it requires excellent depth perception by both horse and rider.

*Never approach a bull from the front, a horse
from the rear, or a fool from any direction.*

— LEON COFFEE, FORMER RODEO BULLFIGHTER

## Q What is the difference between hunter and jumper classes?

A In a hunter class, the judge is looking at the horse's way of going, manners, and jumping form. A calm, mannerly horse is required for this event. In a jumper class, the goal is to clear a series of jumps of varying heights and widths in a prescribed period of time. A highly athletic, bold horse with a strong personality does well at this event.

**Triple bar.** A spread fence using three verticals of graduated height.

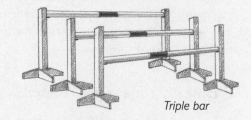

*Triple bar*

**Hogsback.** A three-rail fence in which the middle element is higher than the other two.

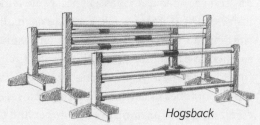

*Hogsback*

**Water jump.** A wide jump over a shallow pool of water — a low hedge or fence usually marks the leading edge of the jump, but in some cases the hedge is placed in the center of the water.

**Combination.** A combination consists of two or three fences of varying types, spaced one or more strides apart. Combinations can be difficult because of the short distance between fences.

# Q What are "faults" in jumping events?

A Faults, or jumping penalties, occur when a horse knocks down a rail with his front or rear feet, refuses a jump, or lands a foot in the water part of the water jump. Normally, the horse is assessed four faults for knocking a rail down. Going beyond the time limit to complete the course also can result in faults. The horse with the fewest jumping and time faults is the winner. If the horse refuses a jump twice or falls during the contest, he is disqualified.

---

### A CLASSY LADY

Touch of Class, an elegant and refined Thoroughbred mare, was an elite jumper. At the 1984 Olympics in Los Angeles, the talented 11-year-old mare carried Joe Fargis to individual and team Gold Medals in show jumping. During the competition, Touch of Class posted the first clear double rounds in Olympic history and, overall, cleared 90 of 91 jumps. She was the first nonhuman to win the U.S. Olympic Committee's Female Equestrian Athlete of the Year Award.

---

# Q How did rodeos get started?

A Today, rodeo describes a contest involving cowboys, cowgirls, horses, calves, steers, bulls, and clowns. It all began in the plains of the Southwest in the late 1800s when vast herds of cattle that had roamed free and propagated during the Civil War years were gathered for shipment east. As the cattle industry grew through the years, so did the number of cowboys and roundups. Naturally, cowboys began competing to determine the best roper and the best rider.

The contests ultimately evolved into the organized events that define the modern rodeo. (See *What events make up a rodeo?*, facing page.) Quarter Horses and Paints are the most common mount, but Mustangs and other breeds also have the agility, quickness, and/or cow sense that are required for these events.

FAST FACT In Spanish, the word *rodeo* means "to round up or gather cattle."

## Q What events make up a rodeo?

A It takes a number of events to make up a traditional rodeo. Here are the most common:

**Bareback riding.** Traditionally, this is the first event of a rodeo. The horse waits in a chute, wearing only a surcingle with a handhold for the cowboy, somewhat like a rigid handle on a suitcase. When the cowboy is ready, the gates fly open and the horse flies out and commences bucking as hard as he can. When the horse's front feet hit the ground, the rider's heels must be in front of the horse's shoulders. If they are not, the cowboy has "missed him out" and is disqualified. He also must keep his free hand in the air throughout the 8-second ride, while pumping his feet up and down the horse's shoulders. If he touches down (touches the horse with his free hand), he is disqualified. Two judges score the horse on how well he bucks and the cowboy on how well he rides.

**Saddle-bronc riding.** This event is judged on the same basis as bareback riding, but the horse wears a special saddle with no saddle horn and a halter with a large rope attached. The cowboy grips the rope in one hand and sits upright in the saddle instead of leaning back like a bareback rider, demonstrating his skill by sweeping his feet and legs from the horse's shoulder to the back of the saddle during the ride.

**Tie-down roping.** This event had its origin in branding calves. A calf is released and the cowboy races after it and ropes it around the neck. The horse stops, bringing the calf to an abrupt halt. The cowboy leaps off, runs to the calf, and wrestles it to the ground while his horse holds the rope taut. He must tie up three of the calf's legs with a small rope called a pigging string and then remount and wait 6 seconds. If the calf kicks free, the cowboy is disqualified. The fastest time wins.

**Team roping.** Treating or branding large animals on the range required the services of two cowboys, one to rope the head or horns, and the other the rear heels. Their horses, facing each other, would back up, causing the animal to fall, and then stand in place, keeping it stretched out on the ground. In rodeo, the header ropes the head or horns and the heeler ropes the rear heels. When the two horses turn to face each other, one in front of the steer and the other behind it, with ropes tight, the run is completed. If the heeler only ropes one of the heels, the team incurs a 5-second penalty.

**Steer wrestling.** A pair of riders chase down a running steer; the hazer's job is to keep the steer running in a straight line so that the wrestler can grab the steer's horns and swing from his horse, landing on his feet. He must bring the steer to a stop by digging his heels into the dirt. He then twists the steer's head around so that it loses its balance and falls to the ground. If he fails to put the steer on the ground, he is disqualified.

*Many of the top barrel-racing horses are Quarter Horse-Thoroughbred crosses.*

**Bull riding.** This is the most dangerous event in rodeo. A braided rope is cinched around the bull's middle and the contestant wraps the free end around his hand. When the gait opens, the bull is free to buck, twist, and turn while the contestant tries to maintain his seat for 8 seconds. Bulls often turn on their dislodged riders and attempt to gore them, so bullfighters dressed as clowns distract the bull until the fallen cowboy is clear of danger. All bull riders wear protective vests and some of them wear helmets, but injuries are common. Judging is much the same as in bareback and saddle-bronc riding, although the bull rider is not required to move his legs in a spurring motion.

**Barrel racing.** This event is strictly reserved for women in Professional Rodeo Cowboys Association (PRCA) -sanctioned rodeos. The barrels are set in a triangular pattern and the contestants race around them in a clover-leaf pattern. If a barrel is knocked down in the course of a run, the contestant is assessed a 5-second penalty. Electronic timers are used to monitor the speed of a run, and winners and losers often are separated by only a hundredth of a second.

## THE BIRTH OF BULLDOGGING

Bill Pickett, a Texas cowboy of black and Indian descent born in 1870, became famous for "bulldogging" steers in rodeos and as part of a Wild West show. Pickett would ride his horse beside a running steer, grasp its horns, and swing off his horse, digging his feet into the ground to bring the animal to a halt. He then gripped the steer's upper lip with his teeth, biting down with such force that the animal dropped to the ground in pain. Pickett was imitating the action of large bulldogs that sometimes were used to subdue rowdy steers, thus the name bulldogging.

Other cowboys followed suit and soon the rodeo event of steer wrestling came into being. Not everyone wanted to bite a steer in the lip, however, so that part of the event was dropped and the cowboy instead twisted the steer's head until it was lying flat on its side.

## Q Are rodeo broncs trained to buck?

**A** Bucking is an equine's instinctive response to feeling a potential predator on his back. Most horses learn early that a rider is not a threat, and they accept being ridden. Some, however, do not. The reasons can be many and varied, including improper training, but some horses simply will not accept a rider. These "born buckers" may become rodeo horses.

To further encourage bucking, a bucking strap is placed around the horse's middle just in front of the rear legs and drawn tight just before the chute is opened. Although fleece-lined, it irritates the horse and causes him to buck higher than he normally would. Care is taken to not tighten the strap too much, because when a horse feels abdominal pain, his reaction is to lie down instead of buck. (See *Why do horses buck and rear?*, page 59.)

**FAST FACT** The saddle on a bucking horse is referred to as the "hurricane deck."

*A bucking bronco might "sunfish" or "swap both ends" when trying to dislodge his rider. This one has "fired with both barrels" and it looks as though the cowboy might be "seeing daylight" on the next bounce. (See* Some Rodeo Jargon, *page 170.)*

## HAT ON THE BED

Rodeo cowboys are a superstitious lot. One of the most notable superstitions is never to place one's hat on a bed. To do so invites bad luck and even physical disaster. No one is quite sure as to the origin of the superstition, but it seems to have been around since cowboys starting wearing their signature hats.

Another superstition involves never kicking a paper cup in the stands of a rodeo arena. Cowboys in competition never wear yellow shirts as that, too, is bad luck. But many rodeo cowgirls and some cowboys wear different-colored socks during competition to bring good luck.

**Q** What bronc bucked his way onto a state license plate?

**A** That would be Steamboat, a famed bucking horse foaled in Wyoming in 1896. When the horse was 3 years old, he was roped, tied down, and gelded. During that rather violent confrontation, a bone in Steamboat's nostril was broken, causing him thereafter to sound something like the whistle on a steamboat when he breathed.

Steamboat bucked with such vigor that he soon found himself as the featured saddle bronc in a rodeo string. In those days, there was no 8-second time limit. Cowboys had to stay aboard until the horse stopped bucking. Few cowboys could do this on Steamboat, but those who did were almost always assured of winning top prize money.

A photo taken in 1903 of Steamboat's high-kicking action became a registered trademark for the state of Wyoming; it appears on the state's license plates and is the official logo for the University of Wyoming athletic teams.

# Some Rodeo Jargon

**Bronc.** Any bareback or saddle horse whose job it is to buck.

**Bull rope.** The rigging that goes around a bull's middle in bull riding. The rope is pulled tight, with the contestant wrapping it around his hand to maintain a firm grip.

**Dog fall.** In steer wrestling, when a steer drops to the arena floor with all four legs beneath him, it is called a dog fall because it resembles a dog lying down. A legitimate fall is when the steer is on his side with all four feet off the ground.

**Eliminator pen.** A group of broncs or bulls at a major rodeo who are noted for their ability to buck off riders.

**Firing with both barrels.** When a horse lashes out with both back feet.

**Flank strap.** The sheepskin-lined strap that goes around the flanks and belly of a bucking horse's body. Its purpose is to stimulate vigorous bucking.

**Pigging (or piggin) string.** A short, light rope with a loop at one end that a calf roper uses to tie down a calf. (See *Two wraps and a hooey*.)

**Pulling leather.** When a bronc rider grabs the saddle to keep from getting bucked off.

**Running the cans.** Another term for barrel racing.

**Suicide wrap.** When a bull rider takes two wraps around his hand with the bull rope. It literally locks his hand in place and poses the risk of serious injury if the rider is unable to free the hand after being bucked off. It is not permitted in modern rodeos.

**Sunfish.** A horse who can leap high into the air and twist the rear portion of his body to the point that one side and part of the belly is "facing the sun."

**Swap ends.** When a bucking horse leaves the ground facing one direction and lands facing the other.

**Two wraps and a hooey.** When a calf roper catches a calf, he must tie three legs. Normally, he does this by putting the loop of the pigging string over one front foot and then wrapping the pigging string around all three, ending with what amounts to a bow knot, called a hooey. The calf must remain tied for 6 seconds after the cowboy remounts his horse and puts slack in the rope around the calf's neck.

## Q What was the Cowboys Turtle Association?

A In 1936, rodeo contestants, who had long felt that they were being exploited by promoters and contractors, organized their ranks to provide a unified voice. They formed the Turtle Association, choosing that name because although they had been slow to act, they were finally willing to stick their necks out. The name was changed to the Rodeo Cowboys Association in 1945, with "professional" added in 1975 to create today's PRCA.

## Q What is cutting?

A A cutting contest displays a horse's ability to remove one cow from a herd and prevent it from returning. The sport traces its roots to the days when communal herds of cattle roamed the vast western and southwestern ranges. Once or twice a year, the cattle were gathered into large holding areas and cowboys from the various ranches would sort them by brand to take them to market.

*A cutting contestant is not allowed to guide his horse with his hands once he has driven the cow clear of the herd. An experienced cutting horse darts back and forth in front of the cow, blocking it from moving forward and following her movements with his own body.*

A modern-day cutting contest bears little resemblance to sorting on the open range, where a cowboy rode into the herd, spotted an animal who bore the brand of his employer, and quietly drove it clear of the herd to a spot where his cohorts were holding a group of cattle together. In competition, the cutter has four helpers, one on each side of the herd and two out front. His goal, to be completed within 2½ minutes, is to select an animal, drive it clear of the herd, and prevent it from returning, which it instinctively tries to do. The two helpers out front put pressure on the cow to encourage it to return to the herd, allowing the cutter's horse to demonstrate his capability in heading off the animal.

## CAMP DRAFTING DOWN UNDER

Camp drafting is a contest developed in Australia in the late 1800s that combines cutting and cow handling. It got its start when cattle were gathered on the range and then driven to a holding area or camp. The next day, riders would separate designated cattle from the herd (mob) and drive (draft) them into a holding area for shipment to market.

In today's competition, the mob is held in a small corral. The contestant rides into the mob and selects a cow to drive clear of the herd and hold at a distance from her companions. Once the contestant feels he has shown his horse to the best possible advantage by preventing the cow from returning to the mob, the gate leading from the small pen is opened. The contestant moves the cow into a larger arena where he must drive her around strategically placed stakes in a figure-eight pattern.

He then drives her the rest of the way down the arena and through a narrow opening between two stakes that simulate the entrance into another holding pen. A judge awards points as to how well the horse works in each phase of the competition.

## Q What is team penning?

A A group of 30 cattle with numbers 0 to 9 on their backs (one number for each group of three) is held at one end of the arena. After drawing a number, each three-member team must race down the arena to the huddled cattle and sort out the three carrying the same number. Then they drive those three away from the herd into a 16- by 24-foot (5 × 7 m) pen through a gate that is 10 feet (3 m) wide.

This is a timed event with the fastest time winning. There normally is a time limit, with teams being disqualified if they don't pen the animals within that limit. In some high-level competitions, the allotted time is as little as 60 seconds.

## Q What is reining?

A The sport of reining demonstrates a horse's agility and skill in executing a series of different movements, patterns, and gaits. As with traditional dressage (see next question), the best pairs work in perfect harmony, with barely visible cues from the rider and immediate, willing responses from the horse. At a minimum, the reining horse must run a distance at speed and slide to a stop; spin in place on his hind legs to both the left and right, and lope through a figure-eight pattern, changing leads with each change of direction. Points are scored for each phase of the pattern.

*When a horse slides to a stop, leaving two parallel lines in the arena surface, he is said to make "a pair of elevens."*

## Q What is dressage?

A Dressage is a discipline considered by many horse people to be the highest level of equine training, based on the classical principles set down by Xenophon (see *The First Horse Whisperer*, page 110). The word itself is a French term that roughly means "training." A dressage contest resembles a combination of ballet and gymnastics, with athletic, talented horses performing sophisticated and complicated movements and maneuvers. The accomplished dressage rider communicates with her horse with subtle movements of the reins and shifts of her body.

Competition in dressage starts at the Introductory Level and moves in degrees of complexity through Training, First, Second, Third, and Fourth Levels. The top riders compete at the Fédération Equestre Internationale (FEI) or International Level, with Grand Prix being the highest. Dressage, along with jumping and three-day eventing, became part of the Olympic Games at Stockholm, Sweden, in 1912.

At the Olympic level, the dressage arena is 60 meters long and 20 meters wide (approximately 66 × 197 feet). The small-size arena for lower levels of competition is 40 meters long and 20 meters wide (66 × 131 feet). A series of letters along the side walls of the arena are used as markers to begin and end certain movements. The letter X designates the center of the arena.

*Dressage can be enjoyed by riders of any level of experience, even without competing. Working on dressage movements improves the skills of the rider and refines the training of the horse.*

With one rider in the ring at a time, dressage tests begin with the rider halting her horse at X and saluting the judge before beginning. Each ride is scored by a judge, who awards points based on how accurately and athletically the horse performs each required movement within each test.

Training a Grand Prix dressage horse is a lengthy process. Top-level dressage horses are often at least 12 years old before reaching their potential. Although horses of all breeds compete at the lower levels, most Grand Prix dressage horses are of Thoroughbred and Warmblood breeding.

FAST FACT **No one is quite sure why, but the letters AFBMCHEK are used to mark off the corners, centerline, and quarterlines in a dressage ring. One handy mnemonic is A Fat Black Mare Can Hardly Ever Kick.**

## OLYMPIC LEVEL (GRAND PRIX) DRESSAGE TESTS

Tests at the highest level of dressage competition include:

**Collected trot and canter.** At the collected gaits, the rider pushes the horse forward with her legs, but contains that movement with her hands. As a result, the horse's head is held high, his body is balanced, and his strides are cadenced, with the propulsion coming from the hindquarters.

**Extended trot and canter.** At the extended gaits, the horse remains balanced, but moves out more freely and at an accelerated pace.

**The trot and canter half pass.** The horse moves both forward and sideways at each stride, crossing the arena on a diagonal line.

**The passage.** The horse trots in slow motion, with a moment of suspension in each stride.

**The piaffe.** The horse trots in place, lifting his knees high.

**Tempi changes.** The horse changes leads at every stride while cantering diagonally across the ring.

**Figure eights.** The horse changes lead with each directional change.

**Pirouettes.** The horse turns on his hindquarters in a 360-degree circle at the canter while remaining in place.

## Q What is combined driving?

A Combined driving is a rapidly growing equine sport that tests the obedience, skill, agility, and endurance of horses hitched to a wheeled conveyance. Drivers compete with single horses or with teams of two or four in three phases of competition:

**Dressage.** Contestants perform a prescribed pattern of movements within the confines of an arena.

**Obstacle.** Contestants negotiate tight turns and maneuvers through and around a series of cones.

**Marathon.** Contestants negotiate a variety of obstacles, including going through water and crossing bridges over a course that might be up to 11 miles (18 km) long. Penalties are incurred for going off course, failing to negotiate obstacles, and striking cones in the obstacle course. The speed with which each phase is negotiated also figures into the judging.

## Q Why are ponies used to play polo?

A The vast majority of horses playing in polo matches are 15 hands or taller, with some reaching 16 hands, so they are not actually ponies

*Polo was first played in Persia some 2,500 years ago and later spread to other countries, including India, where the game became popular with English officers stationed there in the mid-1800s.*

at all. They are called ponies for their body type rather than their height. Because of the need for supreme agility and speed, the polo pony tends to be small and streamlined instead of heavily muscled. Many have a mix of Thoroughbred, Quarter Horse, and Arabian blood. (See *What's the difference between a pony and a horse?*, page 8.)

A polo match is divided into four, six, or eight periods called chukkers (or chukkas), each lasting 7½ minutes. The polo field is 300 yards (274.3 m) long and 160 yards (146.3 m) wide. Teams of four race up and down the field using long mallets to drive a small wooden ball between the goal posts. The fast and furious action quickly tires the horses, who are rotated in and out of the game. In championship competition, some riders have a different horse for each chukker.

## Q What is the difference between English and Western Pleasure classes?

A In a Pleasure class in either style, the judges look for horses that are enjoyable and comfortable to ride. The horse must be calm and mannerly and respond immediately to the rider's cues at all three gaits. While the overall idea is the same, there are some differences between the two styles in the performance of the horses, attire, and method of riding.

Western Pleasure horses are expected walk, trot, and lope quietly, while English Pleasure horses go through their paces with more animation than their counterparts. In some English Pleasure classes, the horses are also asked to do an extended trot or a hand gallop (a faster canter). Requirements vary depending on whether the class is for hunt seat or saddle seat. (See following question and *Which breed is known as the "Peacock of the Show Ring"?*, page 90.)

Western Pleasure competitors can wear a variety of clothing, usually opting for dark pants or jeans and a colorful shirt. In English Pleasure, attire depends on the type of show. Hunt seat riders typically wear tan breeches, tall black boots, and a white shirt, often with a jacket. Saddle seat attire is more formal, with riders wearing dark suits and bowler hats.

**Q** What is hunt seat riding?

**A** Hunt seat is a form of English riding with classes that include jumps as well as classes without jumps. The saddle normally causes the rider to have a more forward seat, which means that the rider's body is canted forward a bit when the horse trots and canters or

---

# Not Your Usual Equine Event

**WHILE THE MAJORITY OF RIDERS** who like to compete choose a traditional sport such as dressage, jumping, barrel racing, or Western pleasure, plenty of equestrians like to take a different trail. Here are some unusual horse sports that you might not be familiar with:

Ski joring. In this event, the horse pulls a skier over a set course. Normally the horse is guided by a rider, but sometimes the skier also handles the lines. In some competitions, which are timed, the skier must maneuver around gates and over jumps. The sport originated in Scandinavian countries as a method of traveling cross-country in winter. Laplanders, for example, traveled on Nordic skis pulled by reindeer. Ski joring moved to the midwestern and western United States with Scandinavian immigrants and many ranch and farm children grew up skimming over snow-packed trails behind a saddle horse.

Cowboy mounted shooting. Not for the faint of heart, CMS features riders dressed in vintage western garb galloping through a course shooting at balloons with pistols. The pistols are loaded with a special type of blank ammunition that will break a balloon without injury to those nearby. Contest winners are determined by the speed at which the course is negotiated and the number of balloons broken. The horses, of course, must be carefully trained to put up with the noise and excitement.

> FAST FACT A horse that is balanced and going forward willingly while the rider maintains light contact with the reins is said to be "on the bit." When the rider releases the reins and lets them be loose, the horse is "on the buckle."

goes over jumps. Generally speaking, the horses demonstrate more impulsion than horses in Western Pleasure classes, but without the animation of their English Pleasure counterparts. The horse is expected to be calm and responsive throughout the class. (See *What is the difference between hunter and jumper classes?*, page 163.)

**Vaulting.** Part of the World Equestrian Games, vaulting involves young contestants doing gymnastic routines on the back of a horse at various gaits. Participants go through a rigorous training regimen before competing. Some vaulters perform on a bareback horse that is cantering in a circle around a handler, while others guide their horses while leaping on and off specially designed saddles. Vaulting often involves more than one human per horse.

**Poker run.** This is more of a social trail ride than a contest as such. At the beginning of the ride, each participant draws one card from the deck. The group then rides to a second point, where another card is drawn. This continues until each rider has drawn five cards. The best poker hand wins the "pot," which comes from entry fees paid by the riders. Often, there is a celebratory party at the end of the ride, where the final card is drawn.

**Western dressage.** A fairly recent development arising from centuries of horsemanship, this discipline focuses on the careful training of the horse and the relationship between horse and rider. As in traditional dressage, the pair is tested through several levels of competition that require executing specific figures with proper quality of movement, e.g., the horse's body must be slightly curved when moving in a circle.

## Q What is a gymkhana?

**A** A gymkhana is an action-oriented event featuring a variety of contests where speed is nearly always a factor. Some of the more common gymkhana classes are:

**Barrel racing.** Riders race around three barrels in a cloverleaf pattern; fastest time wins.

**Egg and spoon.** Riders must ride their horses at whatever gait is called for by the judge without dropping an egg carried on a spoon (no fingers allowed). If the egg falls, the rider is eliminated. The last rider with an egg on her spoon is the winner, with others placed by order of elimination.

**Keyhole race.** The contestant speeds down the arena to a keyhole shape outlined on the ground and must spin the horse around within the circle and race out without touching the white line.

**Pole bending or weaving.** Riders weave through a series of poles in a given pattern, then sprint back to the finish line.

**Ride-a-buck.** Riding bareback, each contestant tucks a dollar bill under her thigh and must follow the judge's directions without losing the dollar bill. The last contestant to keep the bill in place wins all the cash.

*In pole bending, contestants can trot or canter, though the latter requires a well-trained horse that can switch leads every few strides.*

**Some gymkhana contests are a bit more challenging:**

**Monkey in a tree.** One contestant hangs onto a rope at the end of the arena, suspended at the level of a horse's back. The rider races down the arena, coming under the rope so his partner drops on behind the saddle, and they dash back across the line.

**Rescue race.** One contestant waits on foot at one end of the arena while the other races to him from the other end. The person on the ground swings up behind the saddle and they race for the finish.

**Scoop shovel race.** A rider races from the start/finish line to where a companion waits with a rope and a scoop shovel. The rope is wrapped around the saddle horn and the other contestant sits on the scoop shovel and must remain there until dragged across the finish line. In a hide race, a tanned hide is used instead of a scoop shovel.

**Trailer race.** The contest starts with unsaddled horses in trailers. At the starting signal, the contestants unload the horses, saddle and bridle them, and race around a prescribed course. At the finish line, the horse is untacked and reloaded into the trailer. Fastest time from unloading to loading wins.

## Q Does three-day eventing really take three days?

A Three-day eventing comprises three separate contests of equine fitness and ability: cross-country jumping, dressage, and stadium jumping. This combination of events was originally used by the European military to test cavalry horses.

The cross-country phase, where the horse travels a set distance at speed over a series of difficult jumps, determined the horse's ability to negotiate difficult terrain while serving as a courier or in actual battle. The dressage phase ascertained whether the horse had the necessary training, discipline, and elegance to perform well on the parade ground. Stadium jumping, the final event, was included to determine whether the horse remained sound in the wake of the other trials.

*Jumping is just dressage with speed bumps.*

— AUTHOR UNKNOWN

The first official competition for what we now call three-day eventing was held in France in 1902; the sport became part of the Olympic Games in 1912. At first, Olympic competition was limited to male officers on active duty who were mounted on military horses. Nonmilitary males were admitted in 1924 and women have competed since 1964.

Three-day eventing is a popular sport for recreational riders around the world, attracting people who want an all-around experience with their horses. Competition occurs at many different levels of experience and ability. Contests at lower levels, called horse trials, often take just one day, with dressage coming first, followed by the cross-country phase, and then stadium jumping.

FAST FACT Eventing, jumping, and dressage are the only Olympic sports where women and men compete against each other as individuals.

## Q How much weight can a horse pull?

A A well-conditioned pair of draft horses can pull their combined weight and sometimes considerably more. Depending on the breed, a draft horse can weigh anywhere from 1,200 to over 2,000 pounds, and the massive Brabant can top the scales at 3,000 pounds, so that's a lot of pulling power. Most pulling contests are divided into categories by the weight of the horses so that comparably heavy teams compete against each other.

Early pulls involved piling more and more weight on a skid until, through the process of elimination, one team emerged as the winner, and in many places, contests are still determined that way. In 1926, Professor E. V. Collins of Iowa State University designed the draft horse dynamometer, intending to collect data on the pulling power of draft horses. The device quickly made its way into the contest arena.

The machine can be set at certain weight levels, with most contests beginning at 1,500 pounds (680.4 kg). The dynamometer is attached to an immovable object, such as a tractor or truck with the

*A draft team can pull several tons a short distance and can easily manage a full hay wagon or a loaded lumber sledge, as well as large pieces of farm equipment.*

brakes locked, and the pulling team is hitched to the dynamometer. It records whether the team has succeeded or failed in pulling the weight a prescribed distance.

## Q What are draft horse field days?

A Draft horse enthusiasts around the country gather at field days to demonstrate the capabilities of their horses. These events hark back to farm practices that were once the norm and are now coming back into vogue on a small scale. The events are typically held on farms where furrows can be plowed, seeds planted, and hay fields mown. Teams of draft horses do the work hitched to plows, grain seeders, grass mowers, and other equipment. Many of the gatherings also feature threshing machines and corn shredders that demonstrate older methods. (See *All-American Drafts*, page 86.)

## Q Are costumes classes for real?

A In these fun classes, contestants dress themselves and their horses in a costume of their choice. Many classes have a theme, but in others, the costumes are limited only by the contestants' imagination. In Arabian horse classes, for instance, the costumes reflect the colorful trappings for horses and humans favored by people of rank in desert cultures. Other themes might be Native American, medieval, or Halloween.

No matter what the situation, the horses are expected to correctly perform the prescribed gaits. In Arabian classes, the gaits are walk, canter, and hand gallop. Judges score the contestants on both the costume and the horse's performance.

# Airs Above the Ground

THE HIGHEST LEVEL OF DRESSAGE, *haute ecole* (French for "high school") was made famous by the Spanish Riding School of Vienna, Austria, which has performed around the world for many years with its highly trained Lipizzan stallions. In addition to basic dressage movements, haute ecole horses also perform "airs above the ground," which include such difficult movements as the *levade*, the *courbette*, and the *capriole*.

In the levade, the horse elevates his front end at a 45-degree angle and holds that pose. The movement requires great strength and athleticism. In the courbette, the horse stands on his rear legs and moves forward with a series of hops. In the capriole, the horse leaps high into the air while tucking his front legs beneath him and lashing out with his rear legs.

Dressage traces its roots to the European Renaissance, with noblemen showing off the high levels of training their horses had attained. It is generally agreed that the military also promoted dressage in training its horses, but there is disagreement as to whether the "airs above the ground" movements were actually used in battle.

Those who believe they were say that the capriole movement prevented foot soldiers from attacking the mounted fighter from the rear and that with

*One of the most colorful scenes in the horse show world is a class of costumed Arabian horses and riders showing their stuff.*

the courbette, the horse's front feet could strike down a foot soldier. Those who doubt that theory maintain that when a horse rears up or leaps into the air, it is exposing his vulnerable belly to the swords and spears of foot soldiers. Whatever the case, it appears that dressage was utilized both for conditioning and to develop the horse's athletic potential to the maximum. (See *What can Lipizzans do that other breeds can't?*, page 96.)

*Whether or not the capriole was once used as a combat tactic, a magnificent Lipizzan stallion performing one is a spectacular sight. Only the most advanced horses are capable of it.*

## Q What are the gaits in a five-gaited class?

A The five gaits, normally performed by American Saddlebreds, are walk, trot, canter, slow gait, and rack. The walk is a four-beat gait with each foot striking the ground separately; the trot is a diagonal gait, with left front and right rear and right front and left rear moving in synchrony, and the canter is a three-beat gait. These three gaits are performed by all horses. (See *Walk, trot, canter — how do horses get where they're going?*, page 16.)

The American Saddlebred has two additional gaits, the slow gait and rack, in which each foot strikes the ground separately with the knees and hocks raised high. At the slow gait, speed is moderate, but at the command to *Rack on!* the pace increases, with the goal of traveling as fast as possible without losing proper form. (See *What is a "gaited horse"?*, page 18, and *Which breed is known as the "Peacock of the Show Ring"?*, page 90.)

The five-gaited class is the signature event at the World Championship Saddlebred Show held each year in Louisville, Kentucky. As the song "My Old Kentucky Home" booms over the loudspeaker, the contestants in the championship class enter the ring, coming down the ramp into Freedom Hall one at a time. In the horse show world, it is a moment of supreme drama.

## Q What is a "Big Lick" horse?

A This colloquial term was coined in the early 1950s to describe Tennessee Walking Horses who have extremely high leg action in front and compete at the highest levels. To achieve this high-reaching action, special approaches were taken in hoof trimming and shoeing. Trainers found that adding extra weight to the shoes and additional length to the hoof enhanced the animal's natural action. The long hooves delay "breakover," the point at which the foot rotates downward a bit as it leaves the ground, and the extra weight produces an exaggerated effort when lifting a foot, causing it to elevate more than normal.

Although these approaches have been deemed legal and humane, unscrupulous trainers through the years have used less-than-humane approaches to achieve the desired high-reaching action. These practices included applying caustic substances to the skin around the ankles, a practice called "soring," and/or using chains or other devices that are painful to the feet and legs. The idea is to stimulate the horse to raise its legs higher than normal with each stride in an effort to escape the pain.

Those approaches have been outlawed and at most shows efforts are made discover and punish perpetrators. The good news is that even though these methods continue, most Tennessee Walking Horse breeders and trainers spurn inhumane practices. Some shows now offer classes for Tennessee Walking Horses who are unshod or wearing unweighted shoes and therefore moving more naturally. (See *What is a "gaited horse"?*, page 18, and *Can Tennessee Walkers trot and canter?*, page 102.)

## FOOTBALL ON HORSEBACK?

Native American warriors played a game called "buffalo-robe keep-away" that might have been a predecessor to modern football. The 10-rider teams battled over a buffalo robe rolled into a ball. The objective was to drape the robe over goal posts at each end of the field.

Under the rules of the game, opposing riders can leap from their own horses onto the ball carrier's horse in an attempt to wrestle away the prize. If the attacker should fail and fall to the ground, he must catch and remount his own horse before continuing in the contest. Although this no longer is a popular event, it is being resurrected by some tribes as part of a cultural revival.

## Q What is *buzkashi*?

A The goal of this popular game, played in central Asia, is to grab the carcass of a calf or goat from the ground and deposit it in a designated spot while opposing players seek to thwart the effort. The carcass is typically disemboweled, with the head cut off and limbs severed at the knees. It is soaked in water for 24 hours to toughen it before play begins. This rough-and-tumble game is played on a huge field with nothing prohibited except tripping an opponent's horse. Contestants wear heavily padded clothing and carry whips, often held in their teeth, to fend off opponents. Spectators must remain on alert in case the players gallop into the viewing areas.

Both riders and horses are highly trained and skillful. The wiry, tough horses can stop and turn in an instant, and spurt at full speed toward the goal when the rider picks up the calf. They will stand quietly while a rider remounts after being dislodged by an opposing rider.

*Jousting is the state sport of Maryland, so designated in 1962.*

## Jousting: Then and Now

**IN MEDIEVAL TIMES,** jousting was a rough and rugged contest wherein armor-clad knights charged at each other carrying long, heavy oaken lances and tried to unseat each other. The bouts were both sport and preparation for combat. Jousting is believed to have originated in France in the eleventh century, but it flourished throughout Europe into the fifteenth century. Although the lances were blunted, serious injury and even death were frequently the outcome. When gunpowder ended the era of armored combat, jousting pretty much faded from existence.

*Buzkashi is an ancient game that is still popular in Afghanistan and other central Asian countries. It demands tough, agile horses and very skilled and determined riders.*

It has been revived as a sport through the International Jousting Association and the National Jousting Association of the United States, with some alteration to the original rules. The modern approach to jousting emphasizes skill rather than blunt force. The goal is to score points with strategic hits to the upper torso, rather than unseating one's opponent. Modern-day contestants wear protective armor just as their medieval predecessors did. The tips of their lances, however, are made of lightweight wood rather than heavy oak, and a contestant is awarded extra points if the point of his lance shatters when he strikes an opponent's armor.

The National Jousting Association also features a game of skill known as ring jousting, with riders of varying ability levels competing against each other. In these events, the goal is to ride at speed while attempting to spear a series of suspended rings with a lance. The contest is a process of elimination with the winner being determined by the number of rings speared in the least amount of time. If there is a tie, it is broken by placing smaller rings as targets. All types of horses are used in ring jousting, ranging from Shetland ponies for young contestants to Warmbloods and draft horses for adults.

Another jousting contest, tent pegging, traces its roots back to the days when cavalry charged through an enemy camp, creating mayhem by uprooting tent pegs, causing the tents to collapse on the sleeping inhabitants. In modern-day contests, riders gallop across a course and attempt to pick a small wooden target from the ground with the point of their spear or lance.

CHAPTER EIGHT

# WILD HORSES

# Mustangs, Brumbies, and How to Pronounce "Przewalski"

E ons ago, large numbers of truly wild (never domesticated) horses roamed the globe. Changing climatic conditions spelled their doom in some places, while in other parts of the world, humans had the biggest impact, first hunting and then domesticating the horse. Now the few herds that live in North America, Europe, and other parts of the world are feral, meaning that they descended from domestic horses that escaped or were released from captivity. For the horses who survive harsh weather and tough conditions, whether on the range, in the mountains, or on an island, the distinction is moot, as it is for most people. Wild horses will always embody the spirit of freedom.

# Q What happened to all the wild horses?

A Horses (or their prehistoric ancestors) once roamed all over the globe, but by the eighteenth century, only two types of truly wild horses could still be found anywhere in the world. One of them, the Tarpan Horse of the Russian steppes of Eastern Europe, was hunted to extinction shortly thereafter.

The remaining type, called the Przewalski Horse, a native of the mountains and steppes of Mongolia, barely escaped extinction (see *The Last Truly Wild Horse*, next page). A few hundred captive-bred Przewalski Horses survive in zoos and in managed areas where they have been reintroduced. They retain the yellowish-tan body and dark dorsal stripe characteristic of *Eohippus*, the earliest horse. (See *When did horses first appear on earth?*, page 205.)

---

## A WALK ON THE FERAL SIDE

Feral horses live in the wild but are descended from horses who were once domesticated. All herds of so-called "wild horses" in the world today, except the Przewalski Horse of Mongolia, are technically feral, even though they may have roamed free for hundreds of years. This is in contrast to the only true wild equine, the zebra, which has never been domesticated as a species (see *The Last Truly Wild Horse*, next page, and *Are zebras equines?*, page 3).

---

# Q Where do wild horses live in the United States?

A At the turn of the twentieth century, there were an estimated 2 million wild horses in the United States. As of 2009, approximately 33,000 wild horses lived on federal lands in Arizona, California, Colorado, Idaho, Montana, New Mexico, Nevada, Oregon, Utah, and Wyoming. These designated areas are considered able to sustain 27,000 horses, so managing these herds is an ongoing issue for the U.S. Bureau of Land Management (BLM) and other federal agencies.

A few small managed herds also live on islands on the East Coast and in Canada (see *Island Horses*, page 195).

# The Last Truly Wild Horse

**THE PRZEWALSKI** (pronounced *sha-VAL-skee*) Horse is an endangered subspecies (*Equus ferus*) of equine that, like the zebra, has never been successfully domesticated. Native to the Mongolian-Chinese steppes, it is the only remaining genetically wild horse, although it now exists only in captivity. It has 66 chromosomes, while the modern horse has 64. Przewalski Horses live in family groups and behave in ways similar to feral herds.

Colonel Nikolai Przhevalsky (1839–1888), a Polish explorer and naturalist who was curious about these seldom-seen equines, set out in the late 1870s on an expedition to find them. Przhevalsky was able to provide a skull and a hide to scientists at a museum in St. Petersburg, and L. S. Poliakov is credited with making the scientific identification in 1881. The subspecies was named after the colonel, using the Polish spelling of his name.

Przewalski Horses are short and muscular, smaller than most domestic horses, with heavy heads, dun coloring, and short, stiff manes. Although a few horses survived in zoos, in 1969 they were listed as extinct in the wild, due to a combination of interbreeding with domestic horses, being killed by hunters, and changes in their habitat that deprived them of resources necessary to survive.

A successful breeding program started with only 13 horses eventually resulted in the reintroduction of the species to managed areas in Mongolia. They adapted and bred so successfully that their status was reassessed and changed in 2008 from extinct to "critically endangered." As of 2008, there were about 1,500 Przewalski Horses in existence, mostly in zoos and breeding facilities.

## Q Where else in the world are wild horses found?

A Horses at one time roamed over many parts of the world, but today only small feral herds remain in a few places. Some are maintained as tourist attractions because of their long history and special status as cultural icons. Below is a list of some places where horses still run wild:

**Australia.** Horses were introduced by English settlers in 1788, and now Australia has more wild horses than any other country — over 400,000. The presence of the Brumbies, as they are called, is controversial. They are featured on the ten-dollar note, but they are also blamed for having a significant impact on cattle production and on native plants and animals.

**England.** Many thousands of years ago, horses roamed between what is now Europe and the British Isles before the English Channel cut through the land bridge between them. From those ancient herds descend the nine types of ponies that are considered native to the British Isles. Today a few small, semiferal herds of Dartmoor and Exmoor ponies live on nature reserves.

**Ethiopia.** A very small herd of Kondudo horses has been living in the Ethiopian mountains for at least 200 years. It is said that more than 100 years ago, the Emperor Haile Selassie tamed his first horse from that herd when he was a young boy.

**France.** Images of horses in Paleolithic cave paintings give evidence that a herd of small Camargue horses has lived in a wetlands area at the mouth of the Rhone River since prehistoric times. These horses are a protected cultural attraction. Some are ridden and used to manage herds of bulls.

**Japan.** The Misaki pony is a rare breed that is thought to have descended from horses brought to Japan by the Chinese over 2,000 years ago. Considered a national treasure, about 100 individuals live in protected feral herds.

**Namibia.** A herd of 100 to 150 wild horses has lived in the Namibian desert for almost 100 years, trapped in the area by mountains and fenced-in farmland. They are probably descendants of horses brought by South African troops during World War I. The population dropped to about 70 horses in 1999 during a drought, so now in times of need, the animals are fed and watered by local farmers in cooperation with the Environmental Ministry of Namibia.

**New Zealand.** Exmoor ponies imported from England between 1858 and 1875 were crossed with local horses to produce a breed called the Carlyon. Some formed the beginnings of feral bands in the Kaimanawa Ranges, where coloring reminiscent of the original Exmoor ponies can still be seen. By 1996, the population had risen so dramatically that the horses were considered a management problem and an environmental threat. Public opposition thwarted a plan to cull the herds by shooting, with the result that horses are annually mustered and auctioned to the public by the Kaimanawa Wild Horse Preservation Society.

**Portugal.** A remnant band of the ancient Sorraia horse was discovered surviving in the wild in the early 1900s by Portuguese scientist Ruy d'Andrade, who brought them to his ranch. Only a couple hundred individuals exist, mostly in private hands, and the breed is considered endangered.

## Q What animals prey on horses?

**A** Most feral horses are more likely to meet an untimely end through accident or injury than by being eaten, though lions and cheetahs do prey on horses in Africa. In North America, wolves probably preyed on wild equines many years ago, but horses and burros no longer have any large natural predators in most habitats, other than mountain lions that occasionally prey on foals in some parts of the American West.

Believe it or not, highly aggressive Africanized bees can be a serious danger to horses, especially those who are tied up or corralled. Even loose horses aren't necessarily safe, as large numbers of disturbed bees may pursue a fleeing victim for a quarter of a mile or more and sting him to death. The venom itself isn't enough to kill an adult horse, although hundreds of stings are common and can be lethal to a foal or weakened animal. Instead, the bees tend to enter and attack the nose and mouth, causing the membranes to swell until they limit the horse's breathing, potentially causing suffocation.

## Q Can horses swim?

A Horses are naturally able to swim but usually only for short distances without proper conditioning. They move their legs in the water as though trotting or pacing. Many people enjoy riding into a pond or lake and swimming with their horses.

Putting injured horses in specially constructed pools has become popular at many equine training farms and rehabilitation facilities. Swimming allows a horse to exercise muscles, ligaments, bones, and joints without the impact of a foot striking the ground. Proponents of equine swimming maintain that the resistance of the water also provides an aerobic workout that improves respiratory and circulatory systems.

FAST FACT Wild horses will sometimes wade into deep water to escape biting flies and other pests.

## Q What is a Mustang?

A The word "mustang" is a corruption of *mesteño*, the Spanish word for stray. The term can refer to a specific breed of horse with its own registry and more generally to the feral horses who are managed by BLM. Most Mustangs reflect a wide variety of interbreeding since horses brought by the Spanish explorers of the sixteenth century formed the first feral bands in North America. Breeds and types that have added to Mustang bloodlines include Thoroughbreds, Appaloosas, Paints, gaited horses, and drafts. Sizes vary and coat colorations reflect the full range of equine possibilities.

Although the original Spanish blood has been diluted, many Mustangs still exhibit Spanish characteristics. A few small feral herds, living in extremely isolated areas of North America, have been proved through genetic testing to be clearly descended from the original Spanish horses. Among these are the Kiger Mustangs of eastern Oregon, the Pryor Mountain Mustangs of Montana, and the Cerbat Mustangs of Arizona. A number of registries exist to record certain types and bloodlines.

Most bands of Mustangs live in harsh climate conditions in an environment featuring rocky ground with limited feed. Horses with bad hooves, poor leg conformation, or high nutritive requirements often don't survive. As a result, the Mustangs who roam the range are hardy animals who, when domesticated, make excellent mounts for trail riding, trail classes in horse shows, and endurance racing. They are sure-footed and capable of traveling great distances on limited food and water. When herd sizes exceed the level that habitat can support, Mustangs are periodically rounded up and auctioned or placed with private owners. (See *The Adoption Option*, page 202, *When did horses return to the Americas?*, page 211, and *How many horses are there in the United States?*, page 20.)

*Mustangs, the wild horses of the American West, come in all colors. They are small, sturdy, and very hardy.*

WILD HORSES

# Home, Home on the Range

**WILD HORSES LIVE** in small family bands, with generally no more than five mares and typically a single stallion. The family groups spend most of their time grazing, with as much as 10 percent of their non-grazing time spent grooming one another, an intimate and important social activity. When colts reach maturity, the stallion drives his sons away. Groups of colts often form bachelor bands for companionship and protection, moving about together until they are able to claim mares and form their own bands.

The lead mare is at the top of the hierarchy; her role is to take the herd to grazing areas. The stallion yields to the mare until danger arises; then he takes charge in facing the danger or driving the herd to flight. He often allows the lead mare to choose the path of retreat, while he either hangs back or moves to the front of the group to face the perceived danger.

It is commonly believed that all the horses know their place in the hierarchy, although their roles may shift because of age, illness, injury, or the introduction of new members to the band. Some dispute this conventional viewpoint, maintaining that horses may follow an experienced horse, but that does not mean that the experienced horse is actually leading them. Under ordinary circumstances, there is sufficient grass available for the whole herd, so there is no basis for the competition and aggression implied in a rigid pecking order. If the fodder disappears because of abnormal conditions, competition is still not an issue because nobody can find much of anything to eat.

Other knowledgeable observers argue that it is "the nature of the beast" for horses to have a social order in their group. Often when a wild band heads for water, members will travel single file along a trail and align themselves according to status from front to back. Even in domestic settings where horses have an ample supply of food and water, a horse who is lower in status will immediately give way at a feeder when approached by a more dominant horse. (See *Do horses have friends?*, page 57, and *Are horses naturally monogamous or polygamous?*, page 58.)

## Q How did Native Americans capture wild horses?

A Native Americans used tamed horses to chase down wild horses and either rope them or drive them into an enclosure. George Catlin, a painter, historian, and writer, made frequent journeys into unmapped Native American country in the southwestern United States from 1830 to 1836. He described what he saw in *Letters and Notes on the Manners, Customs, and Conditions of North American Indians*, first published in London in 1844.

He wrote that often two or more warriors would function as a relay team, with first one and then the other giving chase on fresh horses until the wild horse tired and could be roped with a lasso made of braided or twisted rawhide. Once the loop was around the wild horse's neck, the warrior tightened it to cut off oxygen.

When the captured horse was "choked down" and in a weakened condition, the warrior dismounted and placed hobbles on the horse's legs. The wild horse would fight against the hobbles until totally exhausted. At that point, the warrior would either lead the horse off to be ridden another day or would jump on his back and ride off.

## Q Do people still round up wild horses?

A In the past, the usual motivation for rounding up bands of wild horses was to remove them from grazing areas where, ranchers maintained, they were eating grass that rightfully belonged to cattle. Horses are extremely vigilant herd animals who react to anything alarming by running away, and herds were commonly chased over distances by helicopters or small planes and trucks until they could be herded into large corrals. This process resulted in exhausted, terrified, and often injured animals.

Today, it is illegal for the general public to round up wild horses in any manner, but the BLM still uses helicopters to gather wild bands. Horse wranglers construct a corral in a strategic area and then build temporary fences that funnel the horses into the enclosure. A helicopter gets the horses moving in the desired direction, and riders on horseback flank the wild ones and keep them moving toward the corral.

*Whether horses or helicopters are used, the process of rounding up and capturing wild horses is stressful for the animals and can be dangerous.*

Once in the corral, the horses are allowed to calm down and are then separated by age and sex. They are loaded onto trucks using safe chutes and taken to BLM-approved holding facilities where they are trained and prepared for adoption.

## Q Who was Wild Horse Annie?

A During the 1930s, it is estimated that over 30 million pounds of wild horsemeat were processed into food for dogs, cats, and chickens. It was often obtained by chasing the wild horses with airplanes and trucks until they fell to the ground exhausted and then trucking them to the slaughterhouse in debilitated condition. Velma B. Johnson (1912–1977) worked as an executive secretary for an insurance broker in Nevada for 40 years. She was known as Wild Horse Annie for her leadership of a grassroots campaign to stop hunters from harvesting wild horses for commercial purposes.

As a result of Ms. Johnson's efforts, a federal law was passed in 1959 that outlawed the use of airplanes and other motorized vehicles to capture wild horses. It also outlawed polluting water holes for the purpose of trapping horses, another favored technique. The bill was known as the Wild Horse Annie Act. Her greatest triumph was the passage in 1971 of the Wild Free-Roaming Horse and Burro Act, which protected the wild horses and burros "from capture, branding, harassment, or death." The act also declared them to be part of the natural system of the public lands, putting them under the supervision of BLM.

## Q Are there too many wild horses in the United States?

A With sufficient food and water and a lack of predators, a herd can double in size in about four years. In the United States, these conditions result in chronic overpopulation on the limited federal lands set aside for herds administered by BLM. The agency removes potentially adoptable horses to reduce the herds to a sustainable size and, along with wild-horse advocacy organizations, sponsors annual adoption days (see *The Adoption Option*, page 202). There are, however, never enough homes for the number of adoptable horses.

The cost of maintaining the excess population of horses is a strain on BLM's budget, and it factors into the discussion about euthanizing some of the horses culled from the wild herd. Euthanasia (from the Greek *eu* meaning good, and *thanatos* meaning death), is intended to be humane, quick, and painless, but it is a controversial option that meets resistance whenever it is proposed. Without some sort of external controls, many wild horses face lingering death from starvation and disease. Animals who wander onto private lands risk being shot by ranchers protecting their grazing land.

Contraceptives have potential for relieving overpopulation in Mustang herds, but long-acting drugs suitable for horses in the wild have yet to be developed. A contraceptive called porcine zona pellucida (PZP) has been used successfully to control the deer population in some areas, and it has been used for horses in contained sanctuaries such as Assateague Island. It is administered with a dart and is good for only a year. Smaller herds can be gathered annually and treated this way, but it is impractical for the large herds on open public lands to be gathered annually for veterinary attention.

## Q How do people study horses in the wild?

A As with most wild animals, the study of wild horses often is done at a distance using binoculars. Horses in the wild exhibit a strong flight response when they sense danger, fleeing when the intruder is still a long distance away. Because many bands have been chased by riders on horseback, wild horses often will flee when a rider is sighted. They can, however, become somewhat habituated to humans if a person is in the vicinity on a regular basis, often permitting a closer approach.

Individuals and teams spend years observing the behavior of a specific herd, recording and learning from the patterns that emerge. Little by little, evidence of typical behavior accumulates, contradictions are examined, and a picture of how horses naturally behave begins to develop.

### HORSES IN THE DESERT

Telane Grayling, a researcher from Potchefstroom University in South Africa, spent years studying the horses in the harsh Namibian desert. Grayling observed that the horses sometimes go as long as 100 hours without drinking. Their diet consists of grass and their own dried dung, which contains fat and protein. They spend much more time grazing than horses living in wetter climates with more abundant food, and they sleep much less, averaging four hours a night compared with about seven hours for a domestic horse.

## THE ADOPTION OPTION

The BLM rounds up groups of horses and burros from its managed herds and offers them for adoption on a number of specific days and places around the country during the year. To qualify, potential owners must prove that they have adequate facilities and that they plan to keep the animal within the United States. A small adoption fee is usually required and the number of animals that can be adopted by an individual is limited. After a year, ownership officially passes to the adopter. Guidelines for adoption and dates of adoption days can be found on the Bureau's website.

## Q Are horses still sent to the glue factory?

A Before the development of synthetic glue, a key ingredient in glue was animal connective tissue, which was often obtained from dead horses, both wild and unwanted domestic ones. Horse meat was also processed into pet food. As the horse population dwindled, the horse meat in pet food was replaced with by-products from other slaughtered animals and, as a result, many horse-slaughter plants in the United States closed. Ultimately, only two remained in Texas, and they concentrated on sending processed horse meat to countries in Europe and Asia. The last American horse-slaughter plants closed in 2007, primarily as the result of public pressure on governmental officials. Horse slaughter, however, continues in Canada and Mexico.

# Wild Horse Stampede

HORSES ARE PREY ANIMALS, and when they sense danger, their
instinctive reaction is to flee. In the days when hundreds of thousands
of horses roamed the land, when a huge herd took flight it could prove
ominous for anyone or anything in its path. C. A. Murray, an Englishman
who traveled across America between 1834 and 1836, provided an
eyewitness account of a stampede that occurred one night. The riding
horses had been tied up for the night, and he thought he heard thunder
in the distance.

"As it [the thunder] approached, it became mixed with the howl-
ing of all the dogs in the encampment, and with the shouts and
yells of the Indians; in coming nearer, it rose high above those
accompaniments, and resembled the lashing of a heavy surf upon
a beach; on and on it rolled toward us, and partly from my own
hearing, partly from the hurried words and actions of the tenants
of our lodge, I gathered it must be the fierce uncontrolled gallop
of thousands of panic-stricken horses; as this living torrent drew
nigh, I sprang to the front of the tent, seized my favorite riding
mare, and in addition to the hobbles which confined her, twisted
the long lariett [sic] round her forelegs, then led her immediately
in front of the fire, hoping that the excited and maddened flood
of horses would divide and pass on each side of it.

"As the galloping mass drew nigh, our horses began to snort,
prick up their ears, then to tremble; and when it burst upon us,
they became completely ungovernable from terror; all broke loose
and joined their affrighted companions, except my mare which
struggled with the fury of a wild beast, and I only retained her
by using all my strength, and at last throwing her on her side.
On went the maddened troop, trampling, in their headlong speed,
over skins, dried meat, etc., and throwing down some of the
smaller tents. They were soon lost in the darkness of the night,
and in the wildness of the prairie . . ."

# THE HISTORICAL HORSE

## Horses and Humans Go Way Back

In the beginning, the horse was just another source of food and hide, but the course of human history was transformed as various cultures learned to harness the power of the equine. Warriors on horseback conquered warriors on foot, and horses provided the means to trade with distant peoples. Most likely beginning in central Asia and spreading to the cities along the silk routes in Eurasia, the use of horses as beasts of burden and the means of transportation, expansion, and conquest spread around the world, changing history forever.

# Q When did horses first appear on earth?

A Fossilized horse bones have been found in many parts of the world, enabling paleozoologists to trace a more complete history of the development of the modern horse than has been possible for any other animal. The earliest ancestor of the horse appeared during the Eocene epoch, which began about 55 million years ago. It was identified from a fossilized partial skeleton found in 1841 in England.

*Eohippus,* or "dawn horse," was quite small, about 8 inches high (20.3 cm) and 2 feet long (61 cm), and weighed approximately 55 pounds (25 kg). It had four toes on its front legs, while the longer back legs had three. *Eohippus,* also known as *Hyracotherium,* lived mainly in the forests of the North American West and in Europe, and to a lesser extent in Asia and Africa. Based on the structure of its teeth and jaw, it apparently fed on low-growing branches and shrubs.

*Mesohippus,* or "middle horse," was identified from fossils found in Colorado, on the Great Plains, and in Canada, dating its evolution to between 37 and 32 million years ago. It stood 24 inches (61 cm) tall, with longer legs than *Eohippus,* and had three toes on each foot, but put most of its weight on the middle toe.

*Parahippus* appeared early in the Oligocene epoch, which began approximately 34 million years ago. It was larger than *Mesohippus,* the size of a German Shepherd, with longer legs and a longer face. Its teeth had begun to adapt to eating grass rather than leaves, and it had three toes, but the side toes were very small and barely touched the ground.

*Merychippus* evolved approximately 25 million years ago. It was 36 inches (91 cm) tall and still had three toes on all four feet. It had long legs to outrun predators on the open, grassy plains where it lived and grazed. Its face was more like a modern horse's, and the shape of its teeth made it the first true grazing horse.

*Pliohippus* dates from about 23 million years ago, when the Antarctic ice cap started melting, creating a warmer climate than that of the epochs before or after. Standing about 48 inches (122 cm) tall, *Pliohippus* had developed a single toe (hoof).

# Horses Disappear from North America

SOME 25,000 YEARS AGO, the horse was one of the most plentiful animals in North America, and large populations of horses existed in Europe and Asia. Then, sometime after the end of the last Ice Age, between about 10,000 and 5,000 years ago, *Equus* disappeared from North and South America.

Scientists have speculated about a catastrophic epidemic — a virus, insect plague, or some other disease — but it is more likely that horses and other large mammals in North and South America were killed off by climatic changes that caused changes in vegetation. Fossil evidence indicates that before becoming extinct, horses diminished in size by 12 percent, perhaps in response to the shortage of food. Radiocarbon dating of the fossilized bones of mature animals found in Alaska suggests that horses became extinct nearly 600 years before there is any clear evidence of human hunters in the region.

This discredits an earlier theory that overhunting contributed to the extinction. Most likely, as the arid steppes became warmer and moister, less-palatable plants replaced the native grasses and sedges on which horses relied. Because horses need to graze almost constantly and breed only once a year, they decreased in size as they struggled to survive, eventually dying out.

FAST FACT There were no horses in North America from the end of the Pleistocene Ice Age until they were reintroduced by Columbus and the Spanish conquistadors in the fifteenth century.

*Dinohippus* appears to have been an intermediate evolutionary step between *Pliohippus* and *Equus*. It was the first ancestor to show the beginnings of the stay apparatus, the bones and tendons

**FAST FACT** **Several species of rhinoceros once lived in North America along with as many as a dozen species of horses.**

that allow the modern horse to lock his legs and sleep standing up.

*Plesippus,* which developed after *Dinohippus*, was a very close relative of the present-day horse. Fossils found in Idaho that date from about 3.5 million years ago are considered the oldest remains of the genus *Equus*. *Plesippus* was about 48 inches (122 cm) tall and weighed approximately 935 pounds (424 kg).

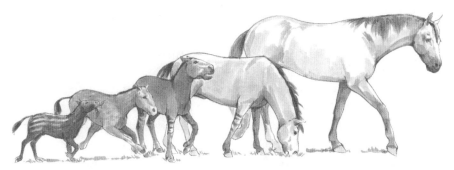

Eohippus  Mesohippus  Merychippus    Pliohippus       Equus

## Q When were horses first used as domestic animals?

A True domestication involves a long-term commitment to care for animals, and it implies some form of controlled breeding and herd maintenance. Before this happened with horses, people undoubtedly captured and "tamed" wild horses and foals, leading them as pack animals and then releasing them when their work was done. Evidence shows that nomadic people on the Eurasian steppes in Central Asia domesticated dogs, cows, sheep, and goats many thousands of years ago, and they surely would have recognized the usefulness of larger animals to carry their belongings as they moved from place to place.

Because large herds of horses were common in that area and were hunted for food, local people must have been familiar with equine behavior. They would have observed their social behavior and realized that most horses have a submissive nature and instinctively follow a leader. That awareness probably inspired local hunters to capture and subdue horses, realizing they could be much more useful than a mere source of meat and hides.

Very little direct evidence exists for when the domestication of horses began. Some of the earliest evidence of taming horses may be a large cache of horse bones and teeth recovered from the central Eurasian steppes at sites dating from as far back as 6000 BCE. Though sometimes claimed as early evidence of domestication, these remains may simply be from horses hunted and killed for meat.

Circumstantial evidence of the domestication of horses exists in fossilized teeth of early horses, dating from about 5000 BCE, found in what is now northern Kazakhstan. Scientists believe that wear on those teeth could have come from contact with a bit or some other mouthpiece. The remains of posts arranged in a circle, as they would be for a corral, and high levels of phosphorus in the soil samples from inside the circular area (10 times as high as the levels in the soils outside the settlement) strongly suggest that manure from captive horses enriched the soil.

The posts are considered evidence of permanent settlements established by the Botai people, who most likely sustained themselves through the cold winters by eating horse meat. Analysis of residue in Botai pottery found traces of fats from mare's milk; horse meat and mare's milk are still parts of the traditional diet of the people in that area.

Another sign of domestication is that variations in the color of horses' coats began to appear around 3000 BCE. Scientists reason that color variation resulted from the crossbreeding of horses from differ-ent herds that were housed together in some sort of domestic situa-tion, suggesting that domestication began somewhat earlier.

## Q Who was the first person to ride a horse?

A It's impossible to know who first decided that horses could be ridden instead of eaten or used as pack animals, but some historians focus on the Scythians, an ancient nomadic pastoralist tribe from the vast area of central Asia that now includes southern Russia and the Ukraine. Beginning around 1000 BCE, their mounted warriors apparently ventured north and westward, raiding and pillaging as they went, until they reached the Ukraine steppe.

The Scythians ultimately controlled central Asia from the foot of the Carpathians to Mongolia and settled in the Ukraine, where a huge sea of grass offered plenty of grazing for their herds of horses and cattle. Based on gold work and other evidence found in the area's burial mounds, the tribe prospered between 550 and 331 BCE. Left behind to help tell their story are lavish tombs outfitted for the next world, sometimes complete with representations of horses and grooms.

## WOMEN WARRIORS

Victorian ladies may have ridden sidesaddle, but evidence from Scythian tombs shows that some of the tribe's best riders and most fearsome warriors were women. Roman historians reported that women warriors faced off against the Roman legions in Albania.

In historical accounts concerning Native Americans, feats of horsemanship and victories in battle generally were reserved for males, but stories exist of skilled horsemanship on the part of women as well. Captain Randolph B. March, a distinguished U.S. Army officer and highly respected chronicler of western history, wrote in his journal in the early 1850s that he observed two young Comanche women set out after a herd of antelope on horseback. According to his report, the women carried lariats and each roped an antelope. Painter Albert Jacob Miller, who spent time in the West during the late 1830s, depicted women on horseback hunting buffalo.

## Q Who were the best riders in history?

A Although many cultures have produced fine riders, the top honor probably goes to the Huns, who swept out of Asia and across Europe around 370 CE and were a force to be reckoned with well into the next century. The most famous of them all was Attila (406–453 CE). Some historians credit the Huns with inventing the stirrup, and stories were told of them standing in the saddle at a dead run while firing arrows in all directions with deadly accuracy.

The Huns carried reflex bows, the most powerful weapon then known, and could kill an opponent at 150 yards (137 m) or more. Their horses were small, fast, and fearless, just like their riders. The horses lived off the land as did the warriors, who raided, killed, and pillaged as they went.

The Huns did not develop into great riders by accident. Almost literally, they grew up on horseback. Children learned to ride at about the age of 3. By age 5 they were said to be able to shoot a bow and arrow while riding. Here is how Roman historian Ammianus Marcellinus, writing in 395 CE, describes the Huns: "There is not a person in the whole nation who cannot remain on his horse day and night. On horseback, they buy and sell, they take their meat and drink, and there they recline on the narrow neck of their steed, and yield to sleep. . . . And when any deliberation is to take place on any weighty matter, they all hold their common council on horseback."

The Hun army traveled with hundreds of extra horses, as many as 30 per warrior. To fool their enemies, they sometimes mounted dummy soldiers on the extra horses. They also used spare horses to provide milk and meat as they conducted their war campaigns.

# Q Did Genghis Khan invent the first Pony Express?

**A** A strong case can be made that the first mounted postal service was established in Mongolia by Genghis Khan in 1234. Genghis Khan and his huge army ruled a land that stretched from China's Yellow Sea to the Mediterranean. Genghis Khan believed that fast dissemination of information was a requisite for the successful administration of his empire, so he established a horseback courier service that operated around the clock in all seasons. There were even different classes of postal service.

Second-class mail was carried on foot. For first-class mail, a series of courier stations located 18.6 miles (30 km) apart housed horses that were ridden in relays across the realm. The stations were staffed by herders who occupied the station with their family and flocks for a specified term of service.

The ruler's personal mail and other urgent messages were carried by a single rider who changed horses along the way. He rode at top speed, blowing a horn as he approached a station to signal his urgent need for a horse to be ready and waiting when he arrived. The couriers didn't worry about being attacked on their rides because Genghis Khan had declared it a crime to harm a rider, and would-be robbers knew that retribution would be swift and final.

When Marco Polo visited the empire, he marveled at the speed with which the couriers crossed the country. It is estimated that 100,000 horses were used in the courier service. (See *How did the Pony Express work?*, page 221.)

# Q When did horses return to the Americas?

**A** The return began as a trickle, which turned into a flood. The first horses were brought to the New World by Christopher Columbus — actually to islands in the Caribbean, as he didn't reach the American continent until his fourth voyage. On his first journey, Columbus listed the following animals on board his ships: 6 mares, 4 jackasses, 2 female donkeys, 4 bull calves, 2 heifers, 100 sheep and goats, 80 boars, and 20 sows.

During his second voyage, he brought more horses, as did the Spanish ships that followed, including conquistadors such as Hernando Cortez, who landed in 1519 in what is now Santa Cruz, Mexico, with a flotilla that included a small contingent of horses. Although we can learn some things about the Cortez horses from written records, we know little about bloodlines or type. We do know that there were sixteen horses; five mares and eleven stallions. Eight of the horses were described as bay or sorrel, two brown, three gray, one black, and two spotted. As the Spaniards expanded their new world empire, they brought more and more horses from Spain and began breeding programs.

On the eastern seaboard, settlers of Jamestown, Virginia, brought horses with them in 1609. A famine that winter led to the horses being eaten for food. Other horses arrived shortly thereafter and were used primarily for agricultural work and transportation. Horses in the colonies roamed freely and their numbers expanded from indiscriminate breeding, as well as through more importations and some planned breeding programs.

In the mid- to late 1700s, many European farmers emigrated to the colonies, bringing draft horses with them. These horses caught on quickly with the American colonists as farms expanded and new areas were opened to settlement. Until the arrival of draft horses, most farmers had relied on oxen to till the soil and harvest crops. They soon found that horses were nearly as powerful as oxen but walked faster, and in the late 1800s and early 1900s, thousands of draft horses were imported by the U.S. agricultural community. The imports included Percherons from France, Shires from England, Belgians from Belgium, and Clydesdales from Scotland.

FAST FACT **Of the 50 commemorative state quarters issued by the U.S. Mint, four feature horses as part of their design: Delaware, Kentucky, Nevada, and Wyoming.**

By 1920, a land that had been bereft of horses for centuries was home to some 20 million head. (See *Horses Disappear from North America*, page 206, *What is a Mustang?*, page 195, and *How many horses are there in the United States?*, page 20.)

## HORSEPOWER ALL THE WAY

That horses were so important to humans for so many centuries is clear from the way we measure the power of the internal combustion engine, which still runs our trains (once called iron horses) and automobiles (the horseless carriage). The term "horsepower," coined by inventor James Watt, refers to the amount of power needed to lift 550 pounds (250 kg) to a height of 1 foot (0.3 m) in 1 second. Watt calculated his new unit of power based on his observations of mining ponies.

## Q What are the horse latitudes?

A The term "horse latitudes" describes a portion of the long journey by ship from Spain to the Americas. Sometimes the trip could be made in a couple of weeks, but without sufficient wind it could last much longer.

Horses being transported had little room to move about. They were tied on deck, sometimes supported by slings to help them to maintain balance in rough seas. More valuable horses might be placed under an overhang for shelter, while others had no such protection from the elements.

In the stretches of water at about 30 degrees latitude, where the wind often didn't blow and the ships lay becalmed in intense heat on a glassy sea, horses often died of thirst and exposure and were dumped overboard, giving rise to the term.

## Q Which culture invented the chariot?

A Chariots were an important implement of war and are believed to have originated in Mesopotamia in about 2000 BCE. The earliest versions were rather cumbersome wagons with wooden wheels, pulled by oxen or donkeys. As the use of horses increased, chariots became lighter and more maneuverable and featured metal wheels with spokes.

*Although the Romans didn't use the chariot in warfare, they loved chariot racing, with the prime venue being Circus Maximus in Rome. Chariots also were used for ceremonial purposes in Rome and other governmental centers in the civilized world, with as many as 10 horses hitched to a single chariot.*

## The Age of Chivalry

**KNIGHTHOOD WAS IN VOGUE** through much of the Middle Ages, beginning in the late 900s and lasting into the 1500s. Knights were professional soldiers who, in most cases, offered their services to feudal lords in return for money and land of their own. After body armor was invented in Persia in the 1400s, the Europeans adopted the idea. When a knight went into battle, he had to be mounted on a powerful horse, as both rider and horse were encased in armor that weighed over 100 pounds (45 kg). The horses were, in essence, tanks on legs.

A knight's training began at an early age, often as young as seven, when he became a page. He retained that status until about age 14, when he was elevated to squire, which amounted to being a knight's assistant. From 14 to 21, the youth honed his riding and fighting skills until he was declared a knight. Knighthood wasn't possible for the poorer classes because a knight had to furnish his own horses and expensive equipment.

A knight needed different types of horses for different tasks. His warhorse, or **destrier**, was a type of horse, rather than a specific breed. The destrier, usually a stallion, was large and powerful as well as agile. They most likely were a bit lighter than modern-day draft horses, comparable to an Andalusian, Holsteiner, or Trakehner.

The chariot was a simple device, with a flat floor large enough to hold two people. A curved metal barrier at the front end provided some protection from arrows for the occupants. Each soldier in the chariot also carried a shield. When used in combat, one soldier drove the horses and the second was usually an archer, armed with a short, powerful bow. The chariot was pulled by either two or four horses hitched abreast. It remained an important implement of war for about two centuries before being replaced by cavalry units.

When hunting, the knight was mounted on a fast horse, known as a **courser**, comparable to today's Thoroughbred. When traveling, he used a calm horse called a **palfrey**, a hardy and smooth-traveling horse who often contained Barb and Arabian blood. When traveling to battle or a tournament, the knight would be inclined to ride his palfrey and lead his destrier because of the palfrey's smoother gait. His baggage would be borne by a horse known as a **sumpter**, a small, rather muscular animal capable of carrying heavy loads.

*Mounted on his tall warhorse, the knight could look down on the peasants on foot, perhaps giving rise to the phrase "on his high horse."*

# Q What is a vaquero?

A In Mexico, *vaquero* is synonymous with "cowboy" in the United States. When the Spanish reintroduced the horse and then cattle to the North American continent beginning in 1519, cattle and horses were pretty much allowed to run free and breed at will. It soon became clear that someone would have to tend to the burgeoning cattle herds. The answer was riders on horseback.

The Spanish landowners did not look on tending cattle as noble work, but rather as common labor, so they solicited the help of poor natives, blacks, or other non-Spaniards, who were called vaqueros. The vaqueros adopted a style of dress unique to their vocation. The hot sun demanded shade for head and face, giving rise to the sombrero, with its low flat crown and broad brim. The vaquero often rode through thorn-filled country, so he wore heavy leather pants, a precursor to chaps. Often, the leather pants were held in place by a colorful sash that kept the midsection warm during cold weather. In the beginning, many vaqueros went barefoot, especially those working in warmer regions. Almost all of them wore spurs, even if they had to be strapped onto bare ankles.

In the early days of cattle breeding in Mexico, animals were slaughtered for their hides, which were sent back to Europe, rather than for the meat. The vaquero carried a long lance with which he hamstrung the animal by severing the tendons in a rear leg. The rider then dismounted and dispatched the crippled beast with the same blade.

FAST FACT "Piebald" describes a black and white coat pattern. A "skewbald" horse combines white with any color other than black (chestnut, palomino, bay, buckskin).

As the human population grew, the demand for beef increased and vaqueros had to adapt to meet the needs of the time. They had to be well mounted and be skilled riders to move large herds of cattle across great distances. Horns were added to saddles and vaqueros became experts with the lariat so that cattle could be captured but not crippled. The horse-training skills they developed passed from father to son and are still practiced today.

As Mexican cattle moved north into what is now Texas, cattle and people from the eastern United States moved south into the same area, and the cultures met and merged. The American cowboy was born during this era, and much of what became his wardrobe and way of riding was borrowed from the vaquero. (See *Why isn't the opposite of Western riding called "Eastern" riding?*, page 117.)

## Q When did Native Americans become horsemen?

A When the Spanish arrived at what today is Vera Cruz, Mexico, in 1519, they launched an effort to subjugate the native tribes throughout the area. They were highly successful and, in northern Mexico, many of the native Pueblo Indians became serfs or slaves.

In 1680, following years of drought and being ravaged by disease, the Pueblos had had enough, and they revolted all across northern Mexico. The Spanish, including landowners and Catholic clergy from a number of missions, fled to Santa Fe for safety, leaving horses, cattle, and sheep behind.

The Pueblos were happy with their windfall as far as it pertained to sheep. They preferred sheep to horses and cattle because sheep were easier to care for and required less forage. They began trading horses to nearby Apache and Navajo tribes. Those tribes, in turn, began trading horses to tribes farther north. Within a year, horses had made their way to the plains tribes of Texas and then to the tribes in what is now Colorado.

Horse ownership brought about an almost immediate cultural change for many Native American tribes. Until the horse came along, most of them had been hunter-gatherers. They hunted game in the area, but also planted crops. With increased mobility, many became nomadic hunters, moving from camp to camp as they followed the migration of buffalo and other game. Because of their value, a warrior's wealth was calculated by the number of hunting and war horses he owned.

## Catlin on Comanches

GEORGE CATLIN, painter, historian, and writer, traveled through uncharted Native American country between 1830 and 1836. This is one of his accounts of Comanche horsemanship, as recorded in *Letters and Notes on the Manners, Customs, and Conditions of North American Indians,* first published in London in 1844:

"Among their feats of riding, there is one that has astonished me more than anything of the kind I have ever seen, or ever expect to see, in my life: a stratagem of war. Learned and practiced by every young man in the tribe; by which he is able to drop his body upon the side of his horse at the instant he is passing, effectually screened from his enemies' weapons as he [lies] in a horizontal position behind the body of his horse, with his heel hanging over the horse's back;

by which he has the power of throwing himself up again, and changing to the other side of the horse if necessary. In this wonderful condition, he will hang whilst his horse is at fullest speed, carrying with him his bow and his shield, and also his long lance of 14 feet in length, all or either of which he will wield upon his enemy as he passes; rising and throwing his arrows over the horse's back, or with ease and equal success under the horse's neck.

"This astonishing feat which the young men have been repeatedly playing off to our surprise as well as amusement, whilst they have been galloping about in front of our tents, completely puzzled the whole of us and appeared to be the result of magic, rather than of skill acquired by practice. I had several times great curiosity to approach them, to ascertain by what means their bodies could be suspended in this manner, where nothing could be seen but the heel hanging over the horse's back. In these endeavors, I was continually frustrated, until one day I coaxed a young fellow up within a little distance of me, by offering him a few plugs of tobacco, and he in a moment solved the difficulty, as far as to render it apparently more feasible than before; yet leaving it one of the most extraordinary results of practice and persevering endeavors.

"I found on examination, that a short hair halter was passed around under the neck of the horse, and both ends tightly braided into the mane, on the withers, leaving a loop to hang under the neck and against the breast, which, being caught up in his hand, makes a sling into which the elbow falls, taking the weight of the body on the middle of the upper arm. Into this loop he drops suddenly and fearlessly, leaving his heel to hang over the back of the horse to steady, and also to restore him when he wishes to regain his upright position on the horse's back."

## Q Did Lewis and Clark use horses on their expedition?

A The explorers did not have horses in the beginning of their journey in 1804 because they were traveling up the Missouri River by boat. When they reached the Bitterroot Mountains of Montana, they realized it would be impossible to venture farther without horses to carry supplies and serve as mounts for the explorers.

Sacajawea, the young Shoshone wife of a French-Canadian guide working for the expedition, guided the explorers to her tribe, where they obtained 29 horses. The expedition was able to acquire a few more horses from the Flathead Indians in the Bitterroot Valley, for a total of about 40 head.

The horses made it possible for the explorers to cross the mountains, although the expedition became lost and fought snow and cold

||||||||||||||||||||||||||||||||||||||||||||||||||||||||||||||||||||||||||||||||||||||||||||||||||||||

## Lewis on the Nez Perce Horses

MERIWETHER LEWIS, who appreciated good horseflesh, was high in his praise of the Nez Perce horses encountered during the expedition. He had this to say in his journal, which later was published, along with the journals of Captain William Clark, the co-commander of the expedition:

Their horses appear to be of excellent race: they are lofty, eligantly [sic] formed, active and durable: in short, many of them look like English coarsers [sic] and would make a figure in any country. Some of those horses are pided [pied] with large spots of white irregularly scattered and intermixed with the black, brown or bey [bay] or some other dark colour, but the larger portion of them are of an uniform color with stars, snips and white feet, or this rispect [sic] marked much like our best blooded horses in Virginia, which they resemble as well in fleetness as in form and colours.

The natives suffer them to run at large in the plains, the grass of which furnishes them their only subsistence their masters taking no trouble to lay in a winters store for them, but they even keep fat if not much used on the dry grass of the plains during the winter.

||||||||||||||||||||||||||||||||||||||||||||||||||||||||||||||||||||||||||||||||||||||||||||||||||||||

weather along the way. When they ran out of food, a colt was slaughtered. The explorers left 38 horses behind when they continued on toward the ocean in canoes. The horses were left with the Nez Perce Indians, who had befriended the group.

## Q How did the Pony Express work?

A The Pony Express, established in 1860, was designed to replace coast-to-coast mail delivery by stagecoach, which took more than three weeks. A private company, Central Overland California and Pikes Peak Express, purchased some 420 horses and placed them at 190 stations scattered along a 1,966-mile (3,164 km) route that began in St. Joseph, Missouri, and ended in Sacramento, California. The goal was to travel the distance in 10 days.

The developing western horse, which combined eastern blood from the Thoroughbred with Spanish bloodlines, appeared to be the horse of choice for this enterprise, being both fleet of foot and durable. A rider would race across the countryside, arrive at a station, leap from the back of his spent horse, spring onto a fresh one, and gallop off.

The venture lasted until fall 1861, when it closed because the owners were losing money and the telegraph was on its way in. (See *Did Genghis Khan invent the Pony Express?*, page 211.)

*Everything possible was done to lighten the load of a Pony Express horse. The riders, for the most part, were short and wiry, and letters were written on tissue paper. The tack was minimal and the riders wore light boots and clothing and often did not carry a weapon.*

# Q What is a bell mare?

A In the days when goods were transported from one part of the country to another by strings of pack mules, a prime problem was to keep the mules traveling forward without straying. It was impractical to tie them together because a tangle along the line would stop the entire string, costing precious time.

Experienced packers discovered that mules had an affinity for mares; some said gray ones in particular. No one knows why this is true (memories of their mothers, perhaps?), but the revelation was put to good use. Packers would introduce a mare to their string and allow the mules to form an attachment to her. The packer would then tie a bell around the mare's neck and set off on the prescribed route with the mare in front. As long as the string of mules could see the mare or hear her bell, they would follow obediently behind. The scene was immortalized in paintings by both Frederick Remington and Charles M. Russell.

When a camping area was reached at the end of the day, the mules were unloaded and turned free to graze. The bell mare was hobbled to prevent her wandering, and the mules would remain in the vicinity and be ready to continue the journey in the morning. Many modern-day packers who take guests on mountain pack trips with mules still follow the custom of bringing a bell mare along.

# Q Were the Union and Confederate cavalries different in any way?

A In the beginning of the Civil War, the majority of Confederate soldiers were better riders and were better mounted than their Union counterparts. Many wealthy Southern volunteers had access to quality horses and were expected to provide their own horses when joining the cavalry. A downside to this approach was that soldiers were granted a 30-day furlough to go home and secure another mount when their horse was killed or injured.

The North, meanwhile, concentrated much more heavily on infantry and artillery. In the early months of the war, the Union had only six cavalry regiments. By 1863, this had been increased to

35 regiments. The Union's cavalry seemed always to lack mounts, even though the North had nearly twice as many horses.

In the beginning, the Southern cavalry had the upper hand, but as the conflict dragged on, the war of attrition made it difficult for the South to replace horses as fast as they were lost in battle. Estimates vary, but it is believed that about a million horses and mules died during the conflict.

## AN ARMY ON THE HOOF

Feeding horses during a war campaign was a daunting task. According to Mississippi historian Deborah Grace, the daily ration for a Civil War artillery horse was 14 pounds (6.4 kg) of hay and 12 pounds (5.4 kg) of grain. A brigadier general (Grace doesn't mention whether he was from the Union or the Confederacy) reported that it required 800,000 pounds (362,880 kg) of grain and forage daily to feed the military's horses and mules. The feed was transported by wagons, each hauling about a ton (907 kg) of supplies. It took 400 wagonloads daily to meet the equine food requirements.

No wonder Union General William T. Sherman wrote, "Every opportunity at a halt during a march should be taken advantage of to cut grass, wheat, or oats and extraordinary care be taken of the horses upon which everything depends."

## Q Were horses used in twentieth-century warfare?

A Horses served an important role in the armed forces of the world through World War II, both for cavalry and supply trains. In the Boer Wars that were fought from 1899 to 1901, for example, the British, fighting with two South African colonies, sent thousands of horses to the war zone. Their quest for more horses took them to the United States, where they were willing to pay 40 dollars per head, even though many of the horses arrived directly from the range and had no training. Enterprising American cowboys set up shop near purchase stations and offered their services in breaking the horses before they were sent overseas.

A staggering number of horses and mules were employed in World War I by armies on both sides. They were used as cavalry mounts, for pulling artillery caissons, and for hauling wagonloads of ammunition and supplies. Rapid-firing machine guns, barbed-wire fences, and mechanized weapons wreaked havoc on horses and mules during the conflict. No one knows for sure how many animals died in battle, but the number was in the millions. One estimate placed it as high as 8 million.

## Mules: Too Smart to Fight

MULES WERE A VITAL PART OF MILITARY STRATEGY, especially in the Civil War and World War I. The mule, however, was primarily a beast of burden instead of a cavalry charger. The reason was basic: Gifted with a strong sense of survival, mules were more likely to turn and flee from enemy fire than charge into it.

That being said, a story is told in Civil War annals about mules being involved in a Union victory near Chattanooga, Tennessee. It seems Confederate troops were advancing on a Union force in a heavily wooded area, causing fearful Union muleteers to leave their charges behind and flee. The unattended mules also decided to flee, but were confused as to the appropriate direction. They wound up running headlong toward the advancing Confederates.

The view for the Confederates was obstructed by foliage, but they could hear the thunder of hooves and the crashing of brush. They thought the entire Union force was charging and fled the battlefield. In spite of conflicting versions of the story, mule aficionados firmly believe that mules carried the day.

THE HISTORICAL HORSE

The role of horses diminished during World War II as armies became more and more mechanized, but a great many were still involved, especially on the part of the Germans and Russians. Some estimates put the number of horses used by the Germans at 2.75 million, while the Soviets are said to have had 3.5 million horses in their army.

FAST FACT **The last recorded U.S. cavalry charge occurred on January 16, 1942, as American forces fought to prevent the Japanese from capturing the Philippine Islands.**

*With their strength and hardiness, mules played an important role in many wars, though rarely on the front lines.*

# Q Who were the Rough Riders?

A During the Spanish-American War in 1898, President William McKinley, dealing with a depleted army as fallout from the Civil War and the Native American conflicts in the West, issued a call for volunteers to fight the Spanish in Cuba. One of the cavalry regiments, commanded by Colonel Theodore Roosevelt, was known as the Rough Riders. The more than 1,000 men in the unit came from all walks of life, but they had two things in common — they could ride and they could shoot.

Horses were purchased from western ranches for the regiment, but many were untrained and some were of less than high quality. Here is how Roosevelt described them in his memoirs: "Half of the horses of the regiment bucked or possessed some other of the amiable weaknesses incident to horse life on the great ranches, but we had abundance of men who were utterly unmoved by any antic a horse might commit. Every animal was speedily mastered, though a large

---

## END OF THE LINE

The last horse to be issued the U.S. Army brand was Black Jack, foaled January 19, 1947. He grew up to be a handsome black gelding, named after General John J. (Black Jack) Pershing, the supreme commander of American forces in World War I. The gelding became part of the Third Infantry at Fort Meyer, Virginia, and was used primarily as a caparisoned (riderless) horse in funeral processions.

He was viewed by the millions who were glued to their TV sets to watch the funeral procession for President John F. Kennedy. An animated Black Jack pranced along behind the coffin of President Kennedy, his saddle empty and a pair of boots reversed in the stirrups. He also took part in funeral processions for Presidents Lyndon Johnson and Herbert Hoover, as well as General Douglas MacArthur.

Black Jack died February 6, 1976, at the age of 29. His ashes were placed in an urn at a monument to him at Fort Myer, Virginia.

---

number remained to the end mounts upon which an ordinary rider would have felt uncomfortable."

In May 1898, the regiment and their horses moved from their training area near San Antonio, Texas, to Tampa, Florida, for the trip to Cuba. Space problems on ships, however, resulted in many of the men and almost all of the horses being left behind. When Roosevelt led his famous charge of Rough Riders up Kettle Hill and San Juan Hill, he was about the only one mounted. The rest of the Rough Riders fought on foot in the engagement that ended in a U.S. victory.

## Q What was a "cradle on wheels"?

A That's what Mark Twain called the stagecoach after a bouncy trip through the West. Instead of having steel springs to absorb the concussion from rutted, rocky trails, the stagecoach body was suspended on heavy leather straps, called throughbraces. The straps allowed it to sway back and forth rather than bounce up and down, but it was still a rough ride.

*Most stagecoaches were pulled by four-horse teams using what could be described as in-between horses. They were larger than many saddle horses of the day, but smaller than most draft horses, giving them the strength to pull a heavy load at a rapid pace.*

# Horses in Agriculture

HEAVY HORSES bred for farm work are found around the world, and were used for many centuries before modern machinery nearly drove the draft horse to extinction. When North America was first being settled, the pulling of farm implements was pretty much handled by oxen. They were powerful and steady — although slow — and could also be eaten. Their slow pace wasn't a problem in the heavily forested East, where farm plots tended to be fairly small.

But in the nineteenth century, as vast tracts of land were opened for settlement, America became the breadbasket of the world. In some of the Plains states, a single wheat field might cover 500 acres (202 ha). Between 1820 and 1870, a revolution in the agricultural industry resulted in the development of more efficient and larger implements. Some of the huge harvesters that were capable of both cutting wheat and tying it into bundles required 40 horses or mules to pull them.

Farming on this scale created a huge demand for larger draft horses and they were imported by the thousands from Europe. The draft horse developed into a larger animal as breeders sought to produce horses who might tip the scales at 2,000 pounds (907 kg).

The demand for heavy horses waned after World War I and came to an end in the wake of World War II, when tractors and mechanized farm machinery replaced the horse. There were some 95,000 draft horses in America in 1920, but by 1945, that figure had dropped to fewer than 2,000. Today, many small farmers have returned to using actual horse power on their land, sparking a resurgence of interest in these magnificent animals.

Stagecoaches were so named because of the stops at various stages of the journey, where horses could be changed or at least rested. One of the prime functions of the stagecoach was to deliver mail from one part of the country to another. In 1858, the Post Office awarded a mail contract to Butterfield Overland Mail Company. The company was committed to delivering mail from St. Louis to San Francisco, a distance of 2,800 miles (4,506 km), in 25 days.

To launch the operation, the Butterfield Company purchased 100 new Concord stagecoaches, about 1,000 horses, and 500 mules. (See *How did the Pony Express work?*, page 221.) To make the trip in 25 days, a series of stage stations stocked with fresh horses and provisions for the passengers had to be established. The teams left behind were rested and then put back into the rotation.

## Q How were horses used in cities?

A Not everyone could afford to keep a private carriage or hire a hansom cab, so one way horses were used in cities was in mass transit systems. In 1886, some 100,000 horses and mules were being used in more than 500 street railways in 300 American cities. Thousands more were employed to haul wagons loaded with goods that arrived by train and needed to be conveyed to specific destinations. Dairies, breweries, and meat packers used hundreds of teams, ranging from

*The horse-drawn delivery cart was a familiar sight for decades in cities and towns in many parts of the world.*

two- to six-horse hitches, to deliver their goods to the marketplace. Horses also pulled fire trucks.

Mechanization spelled doom for the urban horse as cars and trucks took over. Machines were easier to maintain and didn't produce tons of manure to be cleared from city streets.

## MINDING THE MANURE

The urban horse population in America reached its zenith in the early 1900s, with about 3 million horses laboring in cities. In 1900, Roger Matile, a reporter for the Ledger-Sentinel newspaper, did the math for Chicago and concluded that between 1.2 and 2.4 million pounds (0.5 and 1.1 million kg) of manure and 20,500 gallons (75,593 L) of urine were deposited on the city's streets daily.

Initially, the manure was sold as fertilizer to the farmers who produced hay and oats to feed urban horses. As the number of horses increased, however, the fertilizer market crashed and stables and city officials had to pay to have the manure hauled off. When farmers were busy in the fields, however, they placed the hauling of manure from cities low on their list of priorities. As manure continued to accumulate during these periods, it often was piled on vacant lots, with mounds reaching 40 to 60 feet (12.2–18.3 m) high, and an estimated 3 billion flies hatching daily. (See *In One End and Out the Other*, page 33.)

## Q Who was the first equine movie star?

A One of the first significant Westerns was *The Great Train Robbery*, a silent movie filmed in 1903. The action took place in "the West," but the movie was actually shot in New Jersey. The horses in that film were pretty much bit players, as the movie revolved around tales of outlaws like Jesse James. It wasn't until the cowboy culture took hold of Hollywood that horses became dominant figures in the movies.

One of the first movie cowboys was W. S. Hart, a 49-year-old actor who had played a variety of roles on stages in New York. He came into prominence as a movie cowboy in the early 1900s as he fought against the forces of evil with his spotted horse, Fritz. Hart was among the first to focus attention on his horse as he petted Fritz and showered him with affection. Soon, Fritz was getting equal billing on movie posters. He would be followed through the years by a multitude of equines that graced the silver screen from silent movie days all the way into the 1970s, when Westerns went into decline.

||||||||||||||||||||||||||||||||||||||||||||||||||||||||||||||||||||||||||||||||||||||||||||||||||||||||||||

## The Tom and Tony Show

TOM MIX was a flamboyant character who was a rodeo rider, soldier, and lawman before hitting the silver screen in 1910 and changing forever the image of the movie cowboy. Mix wore a ten-gallon hat and gaudy shirts. Silver adorned the bridle, breast collar and saddle of his equine partner, named Tony. Olive Stokes Mix, who was married to the actor from 1909 to 1917, wrote in her biography that a friend had discovered Tony as a colt tied to a chicken cart traveling down the street in an Arizona town. Others say that Tony was a Morgan raised on a Texas ranch. Whatever his origin, Tony helped carry his rider to fame.

Mix taught Tony some 20 tricks, ranging from untying a rope to bowing, lying down, dancing, nodding, shaking his head, and rearing on command. Tony appeared in his first movie in 1914 and was an instant box-office hit. Before long, his fan mail rivaled that received by Mix.

Mix refused a double for either him or Tony in action scenes, an insistence that almost cost them their lives. In one movie scene, a cache of dynamite was to explode just after Mix and Tony cleared the area. Something went wrong and the dynamite exploded as Tony galloped over it. Horse and rider were buried in the rubble. Olive Stokes Mix wrote that Tony lay quietly until Mix was extricated and only then got to his feet.

Mix starred in 336 films, most of them also featuring Tony. The actor was Tony's only trainer and no one else rode him. When traveling, Tony had his own private railway car.

|||||||||||||||||||||||||||||||||||||||||||||||||||||||||||||||||||||||||||||||||||||||||||||||||||||||||||

## Q How are movie horses trained to fall while galloping?

A In the early days of filmmaking, horses and other animals often were treated as disposable products. If a horse happened to be killed or injured, a replacement was brought in. Falls were produced by trip-wires that flipped the horse in mid-run. A major turning point came in 1939 when the movie *Jesse James* was filmed. In one scene, the star and his horse plunge over a cliff and into a river to escape a posse. The next scene shows them swimming to safety.

In reality the plunge into the river panicked the horse, which drowned. To shoot the scene, the horse was placed on a slippery plat-form called a tilt chute and dumped over the cliff. When word leaked out about the incident, public outrage forced reforms to protect ani-mals in films.

These days, representatives of the American Humane Association (AHA) Film and TV Unit provide a significant presence on almost all movie sets where animals are involved. Their role is to make certain that no animal is mistreated or deliberately injured. Horses can be trained to lie down on cue, but teaching them to fall while running is virtually impossible, so mechanical means are still used. However, filmmakers must follow stringent rules and regulations in preparing safe areas where stunts, such as a horse falling at a gallop, are to be filmed.

In the final scene of *Hidalgo* (released in 2004), featuring a paint horse that wins a marathon race in Arabia, some 570 Montana range horses were filmed galloping across the plains as the victori-ous Hidalgo is set free on a western prairie in the United States. A lot of preparation went into that scene, says Rex Peterson, who trained the five paint horses that were used to portray Hidalgo: "We started teaching them to cross that area 50 at a time, and then we used a group of 100 and just kept adding more. There were a lot of gopher holes in that area and it took a crew two weeks to get everything safe for the horses."

# Diving Horses

**AN ACT IN WHICH HORSES DOVE** off a high platform into a pool of water ran for many years in Atlantic City, New Jersey, beginning in the 1920s at the hugely popular Steel Pier resort and continuing until 1978, when Steel Pier was sold. The horses, with female riders aboard, would leap off a 40-foot platform (sometimes as high as 60 feet) and into 12-foot-deep tank. The act came under fire from animal protection organizations, but individuals involved maintained that the horses were eager to jump and that none were injured.

The diving act was the brainchild of Dr. W. F. Carver, a noted sportsman in the area. The story is told that he was crossing a bridge on horseback one stormy night when the bridge collapsed and rider and horse plunged into a raging river 40 feet below. Dr. Carver was impressed that his horse executed a balanced dive and both swam safely to shore. He set about training horses to dive on cue. The first divers were ridden by his son, Al. However, it was quickly determined that a pretty girl aboard the diving horse had more spectator appeal than a man, and only women rode the divers at Steel Pier from that point on.

One of the first women to ride the divers was Al's wife, Sonora Webster Carver. Riding diving horses was dangerous business for the rider. In one dive in 1931, Sonora landed in the water with such force that she suffered detached retinas in both eyes. Despite the injury, she kept riding diving horses, as did her sister, Annette.

# More Stuff about Horses

## Horse Idioms

Sayings that involve horses have been around for years. In many cases, no one knows when they were first used. Many of the following originated in America, Britain, or Australia.

**Backing the wrong horse.** Betting jargon for placing a bet on a horse who doesn't win the race, which can translate into backing a candidate who fails to win.

**Beating a dead horse.** Continuing debate on an issue that has been settled.

**By shank's mare.** Traveling by foot.

**Champing at the bit.** Eager to start a task or undertaking.

**Changing horses midstream.** Changing one's mind in the midst of a discussion or changing one's course of action.

**Come a cropper.** To fail badly; the original meaning was to fall off a horse.

**A dark horse.** A political candidate about whom the public knows little.

**Don't look a gift horse in the mouth.** Don't check out too closely what has been done for you gratuitously.

**Don't spare the horses.** Go full-bore to get something done, with no slacking in the effort.

**Eating like a horse.** Consuming a large volume of food.

**Full tilt.** Going at top speed, like a charging knight with lance angled to strike.

**Hobbyhorse.** A topic or activity that a person is fixated on.

**Hold your horses.** Stop what you are doing or saying for further evaluation.

**A horse of a different color.** A change in discussion or direction from what is expected.

**Horsefeathers.** Nonsense; ridiculous talk.

**Horse sense.** Common sense.

**Horses for courses.** The appropriate person or approach to accomplish a specific goal.

**Horsing around.** Acting in a fun or silly way.

**On one's high horse.** Having a superior attitude.

**One-horse town.** A very small community.

**Putting the cart before the horse.** Doing something first that would be better served if done later.

**Ride roughshod over.** Proceed without regard for the feelings or needs of others; from the practice of leaving nails protruding when shoeing a horse, to prevent it from slipping.

**Straight from the horse's mouth.** Receiving information from the true source rather than secondhand.

**You can lead a horse to water, but you can't make him drink.** You can give someone an opportunity to follow an appropriate path in word or deed, but you can't force that person to do as you suggest.

# HORSE BREEDS AROUND THE WORLD

Abaco Barb (Bahamas)

Akhal-Teke (Turkmenistan)

American Cream Draft

American Curly Horse

American Indian Horse

American Paint

American Quarter Horse

American Quarter Pony

American Saddlebred

American Shetland Pony

American Walking Pony

Anadolu Pony (Turkey)

Andalusian (Iberian Peninsula)

Appaloosa (United States)

Arabian

Argentine Polo Pony

Australian Stock Horse

Azteca (Mexico)

Basuto or Cape Horse (South Africa)

Bavarian Warmblood (Germany)

Belgian

Belgian Ardennais

Brabant (type of Belgian)

Brumby (Australia)

Camargue (France)

Canadian Cutting Horse

Canadian Horse

Canadian Sport Horse

Caspian (Iran)

Cerbat (United States)

Chickasaw (United States)

Chincoteague Pony (United States)

Cleveland Bay (Great Britain)

Clydesdale (Scotland)

Colorado Rangerbred

Connemara Pony (Ireland)

Costa Rican Saddle Horse

Czech Warmblood

Dales Pony (Great Britain)

Danish Oldenburg

Danish Warmblood

Dartmoor Pony (Great Britain)

Datong (China)

Dutch Warmblood

Exmoor Pony (Great Britain)

Falabella (Argentina)

Fell Pony (Great Britain)

Florida Cracker

Frederiksborg (Denmark)

French Ardennais

Friesian (Netherlands)

Galiceno (Mexico)

Gotland Pony (Sweden)

Gypsy Vanner (Great Britain)

Hackney Horse (Great Britain)

Hackney Pony (Great Britain)

Haflinger (Austria)

Hanoverian (Germany)

Highland Pony (Scotland)
Holsteiner (Germany)
Hungarian Horse
Icelandic Horse
Irish Draught
Irish Hunter
Kentucky Mountain Saddle
  Horse
Kerry Bog Pony (Ireland)
Kiger Mustang (United States)
Lac La Croix Indian Pony (United
  States)
Lipizzan (Spain/Austria)
Lusitano (Portugal)
Mangalarga Marchador (Brazil)
Marwari (India)
McCurdy Plantation Horse
  (United States)
Missouri Fox Trotter
Morgan (United States)
Moroccan Barb
Mustang (United States)
National Show Horse (United
  States)
New Forest Pony (Great Britain)
Newfoundland Pony
Nokota (United States)
North American Spotted Draft
Norwegian Fjord
Oldenburg (Germany)

Paso Fino (Puerto Rico)
Percheron (France)
Peruvian Paso
Pony of the Americas
Pryor Mountain Mustang
  (United States)
Rocky Mountain Horse (United
  States)
Sable Island Horse (Canada)
Selle Francais
Shackleford Banker Pony (United
  States)
Shagya Arabian (Hungary)
Shetland Pony (Great Britain)
Shire (Great Britain)
Single-Footing Horse (United
  States)
Sorraia (Portugal)
Spanish Barb
Spanish Colonial/Mustang
Spanish Jennet
Standardbred (United States)
Suffolk Punch (Great Britain)
Swedish Warmblood
Tennessee Walking Horse
Thoroughbred
Trakehner (Germany)
Welsh Pony
Westphalian (Germany)

# RECOMMENDED READING

No single book can contain the whole world of the horse. There are hundreds of wonderful nonfiction books about horse behavior, riding and training horses, raising and breeding horses, and every other topic imaginable, not to mention the treasure trove of novels and stories that center around this magnificent animal. Here is a brief listing of titles and authors.

## Nonfiction

Anthony, D. W. *The Horse, the Wheel, and Language.* Princeton, NJ: Princeton University Press, 2007.

Boyd, L. and K. A. Houpt. *Przewalski's Horse: The History and Biology of an Endangered Species.* Albany, NY: State University of New York Press, 1994.

Cruise, David and Griffiths Allison. *Wild Horse Annie and the Last of the Mustangs: The Life of Velma Johnston.* New York: Scribner, 2010.

Dobie, J. Frank. *The Mustangs.* Lincoln, NB: Bison Books, 2005.

Hendricks, B. *International Encyclopedia of Horse Breeds.* Norman, OK: University of Oklahoma Press, 1995.

Hillenbrand, Laura. *Seabiscuit, An American Legend.* New York: Ballantine Books, 2002.

Moody, Ralph. *Come On, Seabiscuit.* Lincoln, NB: Bison Books, 2003.

Multiple authors. *Second-Chance Horses.* Lexington, KY: Blood-Horse Publications, 2009.

## Fiction

Bagnold, Enid. *National Velvet* — the famous story of a butcher's daughter who rides her piebald horse to glory

Farley, Walter. *The Black Stallion* and sequels — a boy's wonderful adventures with his magnificent horse

Forster, Logan. *Desert Storm* series — set in the American Southwest; some books available for free download

Grant, K. M. *Blood-Red Horse* and *Green Jasper* — set in the Crusades

Hart, Alison. *The Racing to Freedom* trilogy — about a black jockey in the Civil War era

Henry, Marguerite. All titles — beloved author of many historically based books

James, Will. *Smoky* — a classic tale of a wild horse captured but never tamed

Norton, Andre. *Rebel Spurs* and *Ride Proud, Rebel!* — Two novels about horses during the Civil War and after (latter available for free download)

O'Hara, Mary. *My Friend Flicka* — the first of a trilogy about young Ken McLaughlin, his filly Flicka, and her son Thunderhead

Sandoz, Mari. *The Horsecatcher* — a young Cheyenne boy chooses to chase horses rather than become a warrior

Sewall, Anna. *Black Beauty* — one of the most famous horse stories ever written

Wilson, Diane Lee. Several titles — Historical fiction featuring horses

## GREAT MOVIES ABOUT HORSES

Many classic horse movies come from timeless tales, including some of those mentioned above; others stand on their own as beloved stories. Here are just a few, old and new, that are worth watching.

*Black Beauty* (1994)
*The Black Stallion* (1979)
*Buck* (2010)
*Hidalgo* (2004)
*The Horse in the Gray Flannel Suit* (1968)
*The Horse Whisperer* (1998)
*Into the West* (1993)
*The Little Horse That Could: The Connemara Stallion, Erin Go Bragh* (1996)
*The Man from Snowy River* (1982)
*The Miracle of the White Stallions* (1963)
*Phar Lap* (1984)
*The Rounders* (1964)
*Seabiscuit* (2003)
*Secretariat: The Impossible True Story* (2010)
*Sylvester* (1985)
*Touching Wild Horses* (2002)
*War Horse* (2011)
*Wild Hearts Can't Be Broken* (1991)

# WEBSITES

The Internet is an endless source of everything equine. The websites listed here offer a sampling of the material that is available online. Not listed are individual breed registries, but nearly every established breed has an official website that is easily located.

**University of Oklahoma,** Breeds of Livestock project
Brief descriptions of livestock breeds, including horses, from around the world
*www.ansi.okstate.edu/breeds*

**Horsekeeping with Cherry Hill**
Extensive archives on all aspects of horse care and handling, equine behavior, and stable management
*http://horsekeepingbycherryhill. wordpress.com*

**Jessica Jahiel's Horse-Sense**
Commonsense newsletter and archives covering riding, training, and handling horses
*www.horse-sense.org*

**Horse and Mule Trail Guide USA**
A state-by-state compilation of organized trail rides, horse motels, riding stables, guest ranches and riding trails on state and federal land
*www.horseandmuletrails.com*

**Horse Channel**
The website for horse lovers
*www.horsechannel.com*

**The Equinest**
Blogs, links, general information — promising 100% Horse Crap
*www.theequinest.com*

# HORSE MAGAZINES

A wide variety of print and online magazines offer information and advice on every aspect of the horse world. Here are just a few of them.

*Chronicle of the Horse*
National weekly equestrian magazine with news and results from national and international equestrian competitions, articles, discussion forums, and more
*www.chronofhorse.com*

*Equus*
The horse owner's resource
*www.equusmagazine.com*

*Horse and Rider*
Western training, how-to, advice
*www.horseandrider.com*

*Horse Illustrated*
Promoting the best in horse care, riding and training
*www.horseillustrated.com*

*Practical Horseman*
Expert how-to for English riders
*www.practicalhorsemanmag.com*

*Young Rider*
The magazine for horse and pony lovers
*www.youngrider.com*

*Western Horseman*
One of the leading horse magazines since 1936
*www.westernhorseman.com*

## EQUINE SPORTS ORGANIZATIONS

There is an organization for just about any horse sport you can imagine; this is just a partial listing.

American Hunter and Jumper Foundation
*www.ahjf.org*

American Trail Horse Association
*www.americantrailhorse.com*

The Jockey Club
*www.jockeyclub.com*

Long Riders' Guild
*www.thelongridersguild.com*

National Barrel Horse Association
*www.nbha.com*

National Cutting Horse Association
*www.nchacutting.com*

National Hunter and Jumper Association
*www.nhja.org*

National Jousting Association
*www.nationaljousting.com*

National Pony Express Association
*www.xphomestation.com/npea.html*

National Reining Horse Association
*www.nrha.com*

National Steeplechase Association
*www.nationalsteeplechase.com*

North American Riding for the Handicapped Association
*www.narha.org*

United States Dressage Federation
*www.usdf.org*

United States Equestrian Federation
*www.usef.org*

United States Eventing Association
*www.eventingusa.com*

United States Pony Clubs
*www.ponyclub.org*

United States Team Penning Association
*www.ustpa.com*

United States Trotting Association
*www.ustrotting.com*

Western Dressage Association of America
*www.westerndressageassociation.org*

# INDEX

*italic* = illustration

# Other Books by the Authors

**Les Sellnow**

*Tyger, Wild Stallion of the Badlands*, a semi-factual, semi-fictional book about a young stallion that was set free in the Badlands of North Dakota

*Journey of the Western Horse, From the Spanish Conquest to the Silver Screen*, a history of the western or stock horse from the 1500s to the present.

*Happy Trails, Your Complete Guide to Fun and Safe Trail Riding*, a book on all aspects of trail riding

*Understanding the Young Horse*, a manual on handling the young horse from birth through the early stages of training under saddle

*Understanding Equine Lameness*, a study of lameness problems that can afflict horses

**Carol A. Butler**

Originator and coauthor of the Rutgers University Press animal Q&A series:

- *Do Butterflies Bite?* (with Hazel Davies)
- *Do Bats Drink Blood?* (with Barbara Smith-French)
- *Do Hummingbirds Hum?* (with George West)
- *Why Do Bees Buzz?* (with Elizabeth Capaldi Evans)
- *How Fast Can a Falcon Dive?* (with Peter Capainolo)

*Salt Marshes: A Natural and Unnatural History* (with Judith S. Weis)
*The Divorce Mediation Answer Book* (with Dolores Walker)

# Other Storey Titles You Will Enjoy

*The Horse Behavior Problem Solver*, by Jessica Jahiel.
A friendly, question-and-answer sourcebook to teach readers how to
interpret problems and develop workable solutions.
352 pages. Paper. ISBN 978-1-58017-524-1.

*How to Think Like a Horse*, by Cherry Hill.
Detailed discussions of how horses think, learn, respond to stimuli, and
interpret human behavior — in short, a light on the equine mind.
192 pages. Paper. ISBN 978-1-58017-835-8.

*Ride the Right Horse*, by Yvonne Barteau.
The key to learning the personality of your horse and working with his
strengths.
312 pages. Hardcover with jacket. ISBN 978-1-58017-662-0.

*Storey's Illustrated Guide to 96 Horse Breeds of North America*,
        by Judith Dutson.
A comprehensive encyclopedia filled with full-color photography and in-
depth profiles on 96 horse breeds that call North America home.
416 pages. Paper. ISBN 978-1-58017-612-5.
Hardcover with jacket. ISBN 978-1-58017-613-2.

*What Every Horse Should Know*, by Cherry Hill.
A guide to teaching the skills every horse needs to learn to bring out the
full potential of the horse-human partnership.
192 pages. Paper. ISBN 978-1-60342-713-5.
Hardcover. ISBN 978-1-60342-716-6.

*Zen Mind, Zen Horse*, by Allen J. Hamilton, MD.
Spiritual principles and practical applications of a chi-based approach to
horse-human communication.
320 pages. Paper. ISBN 978-1-60342-565-0.

These and other books from Storey Publishing are available
wherever quality books are sold or by calling 1-800-441-5700.
Visit us at *www.storey.com*.